Japanese Sumo: Q & A

Doreen Simmons
Hiromi Nema

Senshu University Press

Japanese Sumo: Q & A

Doreen Simmons & Hiromi Nema

ISBN987-4-88125-374-8

Published and distributed by Senshu University Press, Tokyo, Japan.
FAX +81-3-3263-4288

PREFACE: WHAT IS SUMO?

Sumo is an unarmed contest between two men in a circular space that is just over four and a half meters across. Unlike many forms of such combat, the generic English term for which is 'wrestling,' the two men cannot circle each other, looking for a weak point; they must come together in a burst of power at the very beginning of the bout. Many forms of wrestling continue on the ground, but a sum bout is over as soon as one man hits the ground or steps out of the circle. The limited space encourages power and speed; it also ensures that the bout is over mostly in a few seconds. The twin requirements of speed and stability have, over the years, produced the sumo body with its characteristic low center of gravity, ideally with short legs and heavy hips and thighs.

Professional sumo is characterized by the ring, by its unique set of rules, both written and unwritten, by its history, its pageantry, and by its special people: besides the wrestlers themselves, there are the referees, judges, callers, hairdressers, trainers, stablemasters, and a host of others who make up the unique world of sumo.

This book assumes that you have already been bitten by the sumo bug. You may have read one or more of the introductory books on sumo that are available in English. This book attempts to fill the gaps, and to give you a ready reference to the finer points. These are accessible in Japanese, but hard to find in English.

Here is an attempt to provide, in a simple question-and-answer form, detailed information on the people of sumo, the physical features, the practices and rules, the clothing, the rewards, financial and otherwise, the beliefs, and the minutiae that are difficult to categorize but we put them in anyway — all grouped into convenient chapters with numbered paragraphs and many cross-references.

FOREWORD

This 'sumo' — Japan's 'kokugi' or national sport that is proudly shown to the world — what kind of sport is it? The people who do sumo are called 'rikishi' —men of strength — what kind of people are they? The place where sumo is contested is called 'dohyo' — literally earth and straw bales; how is its size and shape fixed? Hanging down over the dohyo there is a roof of unusual shape; but there is already a real roof on the building; why is there another, false, roof inside? If you watch sumo on television, if you chat about it on the Internet, this kind of question will doubtless come bubbling up. By now there is a whole shelf of books that give an introduction to sumo, but in English there is very little that fills in the details.

The idea of this book is to give clear, concise explanations of these details in question-and-answer format. Read this book and you, too, can become a sumo expert. Getting a deeper knowledge of sumo, which is one part of Japan's traditional culture, may also give you insights into other aspects of the country's rich cultural heritage. Contrary to what you might think, sumo is constantly adapting itself to changing circumstances (and that is something that makes writing this kind of book a nightmare at times — updates are needed constantly!) but at the same time, sumo goes back a long way, and it is possible to trace certain threads from the earliest artworks and records right up to the present day: for instance, the sumo wrestler has always been dressed only in a form of loincloth. It has been made of various materials and has taken various forms; but its wearer is always recognizable as a sumo wrestler.

For the Japanese enthusiast, sumo is not simply a sport in which one man wins and another loses. Tradition, though not carved in granite, still has a strong influence, and it is easy to feel that we are looking at something from a complex and ancient world. The sumo people may not themselves be entirely conscious of this; and it is this tension between the old and the new, the traditional and the pragmatic, that holds the interest of many of us who come from very different races and cultures.

There is also the human drama: the boy out of junior high school, entering a dirty and sometimes alien world, with everybody around him in a position to order him around, has at first few encouragements; but every small step up brings a lightening of the hardships, and, if he eventually reaches the upper divisions (and many do not), the bright trappings of success. It is, however, a success that depends on continued effort, and both injury and vanity can lead to a disastrous fall.

Professional sumo consists of several different but interlocking worlds that are peopled by different kinds of men, and all of these have their fascination for the observer: the referees, the callers, the coaches, the assistants of various kinds. Surrounding the actual sumo there are also many other occupations that both give and take: the chaya, the small catering companies that appear to be profiting from their monopoly of most of the best seats, act as a buffer in hard times, for when sumo is not at peak popularity, they must still pay for the tickets and take the loss if the customers do not come. A wide variety of sumo souvenirs is necessary, and these need designers and manufacturers — not to mention the wholesalers and the women who run the retail stalls. There is a large informal network of restaurants, bars and geisha houses which also have a symbiotic relationship with sumo; indeed, many successful sumo wrestlers invest their winnings in restaurants with a sumo theme, and also provide jobs for their less successful confreres. There are photographers and artists, broadcasters and writers, film-makers and academics, all of whom make sumo their subject but who also contribute to its popularity or raise its profile in the world.

Finding one's way around this network of sumo connections takes time, and the authors have, indeed, spent time on tracking down people and places.

Last but not least, we would like to express our gratitude to Mr. Shinji Uehara, chief editor of the Senshu University Press, for his generous help in getting this book published.

Note: The manuscript for this book was originally written between 2001 and 2004, but remained unpublished for many years. Some descriptions in the text may be out of date; differences are sometimes briefly pointed out in the notes, if necessary.

CONTENTS

UNIT 1 APPRENTICE

Section 1 SHIN-DESHI (New apprentice)

1.1 How does someone join professional sumo?

Professional sumo is based upon the sumo-beya, commonly translated as 'stable.' To become a rikishi (the preferred name for a professional sumo wrestler) all entrants must enter one or other of the sumo-beya, most of which are in or near Tokyo. At present there are over fifty of them. There is no meaningful 'average size' of a sumo-beya; it can vary from one rikishi to over 40. Only the master of a heya can enter someone on the rolls of the Nihon Sumo Kyokai (Japan Sumo Association, Sumo Kyokai or Kyokai for short).

> Note: As of February 2022, there are 43 stables (sumo-beya), although some are located in Chiba and Ibaraki Prefectures, far from Ryogoku in Tokyo.

1.2 What paperwork is needed?

The master needs certain documents before he can accept an apprentice:

1) Written consent of a parent or guardian
2) Copy of family register or the part of a family register describing the entrant
3) Certificate of health issued by a medical doctor

In the case of foreigners, documents signed by two sponsors are also needed; and they must show their Alien Registration cards (which must be carried by all foreign nationals in Japan) to the Kyokai.

Note: After 2008, non-Japanese entrants need to obtain an entertainer visa.

1.3 Do the boys simply go to a stablemaster and volunteer?

Would-be rikishi can ask a master to accept them, but it is more common for a promising boy to be scouted by a friend or supporter of a stablemaster.

A stablemaster (shisho) can accept any suitable male as an apprentice at any time; but since he is receiving no allowance from the Kyokai for the entrant, he will normally put him in for mae-zumo as soon as possible, that is, the next basho after taking him in.

Note: Since 2010, only one non-Japanese rikishi has been accepted per sumo-beya (stable).

1.4 What are the physical requirements?

They have varied quite a bit over the course of the last century. In fact, as recently as February 2001 the rules were changed again, and for the first time, in a downwards direction. At times there have been slightly different minimum height and weight requirements for those under and over the age of 18, but the growing average size of the Japanese made these largely unnecessary. In general, all entrants must have finished compulsory education (junior high, middle school) and will therefore be aged 15 or 16. In the past ten years college-level entrants have also become increasingly common, and in January 2001, more than a third of the men in the two top divisions had come in from university.

So at the turn of the millennium, the situation was: minimum age 15-16, maximum 23 for those straight from school; and 20-25 for a college or adult amateur entrant. Minimum weight: 75 kg.; minimum height: 173 cm. Both, however, could be waived for a college or amateur entrant whose achievements allowed him to skip the three bottom divisions of sumo. The first case was Tanimura, a short but clever man from Meiji University, who entered Kasugano-beya in November 1995.

Note: Some qualifications of the riskishi entrants have changed slightly since 2001, but qualifications before 2001 remained mostly unchanged.

1.5 Have university men always had special treatment?

Yes, but until the 1970s they were quite a rarity. Before 1966 each college and amateur champion's entry position was decided individually. From 1966 to September 2000, performance in the following four amateur sumo meets was counted:
  1) All-Japan Amateur Championship, finishing in the first 16 places
  2) All-Japan College Championship, a place in the top three
  3) All-Japan Company Championship, a place in the top three
  4) People's Athletic Championship, Youth Class A, a place in the top three

These qualified a man to enter sumo below the lowest makushita level, thus skipping the three bottom divisions. The position was known as makushita tsukedashi, 'attached but outside makushita,' implying that he was outside the framework of the banzuke as his name was not officially listed.

1.6 What are the new mid-term entry qualifications?

If a man has won the All-Japan College Championship and in addition one of the other three, he can start at makushita 10 — 101 places higher than the tsukedashi position (since there are 60 makushita men on east and west). If he has won any one of the Championships he can start at makushita 15.

As before, the stablemaster submits the necessary document(s) to the Kyokai, which gives a ruling on whether the man can be given the privilege. In recent years, many men with college experience have had to begin at maezumo level, at the very bottom; but with their superior experience and greater size, they usually move very swiftly up the ranks until they reach much the same level as those allowed in at the higher position. Not all such men successfully make the transition from amateur to professional, however.

1.7 Is a college background necessary to enter at makushita level?

No; but in practice nearly all the men who come in at this level have been to college, even if they have not graduated.

1.8 What are the new lower height and weight limits?

The new size limits: height, minimum 167 cm., weight 67 kg. Boys in this category are given a set of tests to show their strength and agility. The tests are: strength of hand-grip (measured with a spring attached to a simple meter; all sumo entrants do that, and it remains part of their record); how far they could lob a handball; strength of upward pull (this time a much bigger spring attached to a much bigger meter); how many situps they could do in a measured time; jumping as high as possible from a standing position; moving rapidly with sideways steps across measured lines to test speed and agility; a timed 50-meter dash; and the 'shuttle run' — how many times they could run between two points in a fixed time.

All new recruits are given a physical test (height, weight, heart, blood pressure, breathing capacity, gripping strength, upward pulling strength) by Kokugikan medical staff and oyakata.

1.9 Can a girl or woman be accepted as a sumo apprentice?

Absolutely not. This is clearly stated for all jobs connected with sumo, the basis being the quasi-religious ban on females touching the sacred dohyo.

1.10 Is it possible to be a rikishi without joining a heya?

No. Recruitment can be done only through affiliation with a heya; and if a man leaves a heya he also leaves sumo.

1.11 Is it possible for rikishi to change their heya?

A rikishi cannot move to a different sumo-beya; and one who has quit the world of sumo cannot come back either to the same heya or a different one. If you look carefully at the records of men who appear to have changed their heya, you will find that it is the name of the heya that has changed, not the rikishi. Two heya may have merged, for instance, as in the important case of Fujishima and Futagoyama on February 1, 1993; or a small heya may disappear on the retirement or death of its master and any remaining rikishi may be taken into another; or conversely an oyakata may, with permission, leave his old heya and set up a new one of his own, taking with him some apprentices he has been collecting.

It is, however, possible for gyoji, yobidashi, and those oyakata who are not stable-masters, to change heya, usually at the invitation of the master of a new heya.

Note: As of February 2022, Fujishima beya and Futagoyama beya have no non-Japanese rikishi at all. Instead, Kasugano beya and Tomozuna beya each have two non-Japanese rikishi. Two sumo-beya have emerged into one.

Section 2 MAEZUMO—Preliminary bouts

1. 12 How do new entrants get started in sumo?

When a stablemaster has recruited a new apprentice (shin-deshi), he wants to get him entered on the banzuke-hyo (official ranking list) as soon as possible, so that he can start receiving an allowance for him from the Sumo Association (Kyokai). He gives him some basic training in the heya, and as soon as possible, normally in the next basho, enters his protege for maezumo — literally, preliminary sumo — by enrolling him as a shin-deshi at the Kyokai office.

1. 13 Why is it called 'maezumo'?

The name is said to come from a phrase that is written in the bottom left-hand corner of the banzuke-hyo meaning 'apart from these, there is preliminary sumo on the east and west.' In any case, the maezumo bouts come directly before the advertised jonokuchi bouts on the day's program, with the line on the extreme right of the list of bouts, 'maezumo.'

1.14 When does maezumo take place?

In all basho but that in Osaka, maezumo starts on Tuesday Day 3 of a basho and ends on Friday Day 6. Since March is the time when school-leavers flood in to try their luck, the Osaka basho has to allow more time. Maezumo there starts on Day 2 and continues into the second week.

1.15 Can a makushita entrant fall to sandanme?

Certainly; if he gets make-koshi, that is, a score of less than 4-3 (ranks below juryo fight only seven bouts in a 15-day basho), he will be demoted.

1.16 How is maezumo conducted?

The wakaimono-gashira (Unit 10) are in charge. According to a list they have already prepared, two of them shepherd the boys in on the east and west sides. Since they all sit waiting their turn together, there are no cushions for them and they have to sit on the bare floor. They begin and end by standing in lines and bowing to the dohyo.

If there are large numbers and maezumo is treated as a separate item, two judges from the first shift come in and sit on the east and west sides, but when there are few bouts and maezumo passes almost seamlessly into the advertised jonokuchi bouts, the whole of the first shift is present.

Maezumo presents an opportunity for trainee yobidashi and gyoji to gain experience, and although a young gyoji of about jonidan-kaku begins and ends the series, lower-ranked ones share all the bouts in between, taking turns. The same applies to yobidashi.

The yobidashi call the contestants' names, but standing on the ground at the corners instead of mounting the dohyo. During the bouts they squat at the corners, rising only to call. The gyoji announces the contestants as usual. When the bout is over, the plain-clothes gyoji at the microphone gives just the name of the winner. So one feature of maezumo is that there is no mention of heya affiliation or of home town.

1.17 What is the system?

In principle, a boy has to win three bouts, but if he loses he may take another bout on the same day if there is time. When the numbers are low, a boy may need to go round to the other side of the ring to meet another opponent on his own original side. Since the March 1994 Osaka basho, the number has been reduced to two wins, and in Osaka only, because greater numbers are involved, the boys are divided into A and B and do maezumo on alternate days. In September 2000, an unprecedented situation arose: there was only one entrant, and it looked as if he would not be able to take maezumo; in the nick of time a returnee (one who had fallen off the bottom of the banzuke through sickness or injury) was declared fit to try again, so one single bout was held. September is always the lowest point in recruiting; twice in the 1990s there had been only two contenders.

1.18 Shinjo shusse hiro

The successful boys are presented to the public in this ceremony. In Tokyo, Nagoya and Fukuoka it happens on Sunday Day 8, but in Osaka there are three: ichiban shusse on Day 5, niban shusse on Day 8 or 9, and sanban shusse on Day 12 or 13. The boys who got their two wins (originally three) straight away are presented in the first group; then those who took a little longer in the second; finally, everybody else in the third group, whether they got their two wins or not.

The ceremony takes place when the third shift of judges goes out, towards the end of the sandanme bouts. The boys are dressed by the wakaimono-gashira in kesho-mawashi (2.12) borrowed from a senior. They line up on the dohyo facing forward and go down into a squat. Their names are then read out one by one by the public address announcer and as each boy hears his name, he rises and bows, to generous applause from the fans. When they have all been presented, a young gyoji of jonidan rank, flourishing not his gunbai but a white folding fan borrowed from a yobidashi, announces that these have passed through the maezumo bouts and from the next basho will be entered on the banzuke. With a final 'Give them your favor,' he directs them with curt orders, 'Stand!' 'Bow!' and they bow to the front, turn in place and bow to the east, then the rear, the east, and again to the front. They then descend by the front/west corner (the only time this is used) and are taken by the wakaimono-gashira around the various sumo offices where each one must announce himself with an awkward nod of the head.

Note: The number of shinjo shusse hiro depends on the number of new entrants. There is no fixed number of shinjo shusse hiro.

1. 19 Does anyone miss being presented?

If someone has dropped right off the bottom of the banzuke ranking list, though illness or other absence, and then returns to try his luck again, he has to take maezumo but cannot be publicly presented a second time.

University and amateur sumoists who have been permitted to skip the bottom three divisions and start at the makushita level have already started their public career at the beginning of the basho and they are not presented as newcomers.

1. 20 What happens to the boys when they have passed through maezumo?

For the next six months, they spend six mornings a week in the kyoshujo, the sumo training school, which is the subject of the next section.

Section 3 KYOSHUJO—Sumo training school

1.21 Where and what is the sumo training school?

It is attached to the rear of the Kokugikan in Tokyo. To be precise, it is a long annex built over the roadway along the rear of the building. Roughly two-thirds of the floor space is a long room containing three training rings. The other third is a classroom complete with desks and chairs. At the far end of the training area there are showers and a changing room; at the classroom end, there are offices for the oyakata who are in charge of the school.

The kyoshujo was founded by the Sumo Kyokai in 1957 to provide basic training and classroom instruction for all new rikishi registered with it. Before that, basic training had been left to individual stablemasters.

1.22 Do all new entrants have to attend the school?

In principle, yes; the only exception is made for college and amateur rikishi who are permitted to skip the bottom three divisions and enter at the makushita level (1.5-7). Their standard of sumo is far above that of the new entrants, so they train in their heya; but they have to finish early, shower and dress, and go to the kyoshujo for the classroom lessons.

1.23 How is sumo taught in the school?

The day begins at 7.00 when the boys change into their mawashi (with their name attached to a piece of cloth at the front, for identification) and run around the outside of the building if the weather is fine. Keiko (training) proper is from 7:30

to 9:30 with a short break in the middle.

For complete beginners, all the correct movements of sumo, including the ritual gestures and the sumo techniques, have been broken down into individual parts that are learned separately. These are practised again and again until they become second nature. Especially after the Osaka basho, when there may be a hundred or more new apprentices, the kyoshujo features line upon line of 16-year-olds performing each movement in unison.

After this part of the day, they move on to the practice rings. Beginners have to learn suriashi, moving smoothly without lifting their feet from the ground, and also how to fall properly — hitting the ground with a rolling motion and picking themselves up immediately. The boys are many and the exercise is quickly over, so they line up, take a quick turn in the ring, and join the end of the line again.

As they get more proficient, they spend more time in practice bouts. At any one time there are apprentices at three different levels: the newest entrants, those who entered two months earlier, in the previous basho, and those from the one before that.

1.24 What are the classroom lessons?

Monday:	Physiology
Tuesday:	Shigin, a kind of declamatory poetry recitation
Wednesday:	Calligraphy
Thursday:	Sumo history
Friday:	Sports medicine
Saturday:	Civics (general education)

Tuesday's lesson seems rather far removed from sumo, but it teaches breathing control that is important, and also it gives the boys a start in learning how to sing — a useful social accomplishment. Calligraphy ensures a respectable ability to write with a thick brush in Chinese ink; a successful rikishi will at least need to sign his own autograph in style. Physiology and sports medicine are taught from a very practical point of view, to encourage the boys to use their own bodies to good effect and to advise them on what can go wrong with them.

1.25 Who teaches in the school?

The administrative head of the kyoshujo is a very senior oyakata, and four others under him supervise the actual training. They are assisted by a number of makushita rikishi who are provided free of charge by any heya that is sending a lot of apprentices to the school. These training assistants are men of experience. They may have been up to juryo level, or would have been but for unfortunate injury. The best of them will be candidates for other sumo-related jobs such as wakaimono-gashira, sewanin or managers, (Unit 10) if a vacancy arises before they need to quit sumo.

The classroom lessons are taken by academic teachers, university lecturers or other specialists. As the boys tend to fall asleep in their lesson, the four oyakata-trainers walk around carrying big sticks, with which they occasionally tap a dozing apprentice.

1.26 What happens after lessons and on Sundays?

They all have lunch in the staff cafeteria in the basement of the main building, where, instead of chanko-nabe, they eat such everyday dishes as hash, curry and noodles. But extra rice is provided, and they are encouraged to eat plenty.

After lunch, the deshi return to their own stables where they live as usual, doing chores and waiting upon their seniors.

On Sundays they stay in the heya and live as all the other juniors do.

1.27 Does the school have holidays?

School is suspended during basho time, since the apprentices must all appear for their own bouts as well as helping out with the many jobs that come up during a tournament.

1.28 Are there any other features of the school?

It has photographs of all the oyakata on one wall of the classroom, and the apprentices are expected to memorize them so that they can greet any oyakata on sight; and there are also the Guiding Principles, that must be memorized from a copy hung on the wall of the training room and repeated in chorus every morning.

The Guiding Principles (指導方針):

一　我々は力士の本文である礼儀を重んじます。
1. We will honor the code of manners (reigi) that is the duty of a rikishi.

二　我々は先輩の教えを守り稽古に精進します。
2. We will perform keiko in keeping with what our seniors teach us.

三　我々は服装を正し体の清潔を心掛けます。
3. We will take care to keep our dress and our bodies neat.

UNIT 2 RANKING

Section 1 THE BANZUKE

2.1 What is the banzuke?

The banzuke is the ranking list, published 13 days before each hon-basho, that shows the exact rank of every man and boy officially enrolled in professional sumo. It is divided into six divisions, and the top division is further divided into regular rankers and title-holders. Since very many boys enter sumo at the bottom and very few indeed make it to the very top, the shape is like a pyramid.

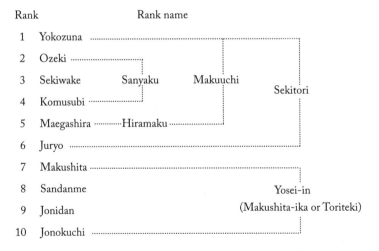

2.2 What are the main classifications of rikishi?

Into sekitori (juryo and above) and toriteki (makushita and below). The official name for the lower rankers is 'rikishi yosei-in' but it is not used in conversation. The commonest expression for all those below the sekitori ranks is 'makushita ika' —makushita and below, although since makushita means literally 'below the curtain' the one word is often used to include all junior rikishi right down to jonokuchi.

2.3 Must there always be at least one yokozuna?

No, there have been cases where there was none at all on the banzuke. The Sumo Kyokai prefers to have at least two, however, so that there is a yokozuna dohyo-iri (Unit 12.2) from both east and west; but unless a man satisfies the requirements for promotion, he cannot be made yokozuna. There have been cases when a man was promoted too quickly (notably Futahaguro) and the two-consecutive-yusho rule (Unit 13.4) is enforced quite strictly now.

2.4 Must there always be at least one ozeki?

According to the rules, there must. If for any reason there is no real ozeki on the banzuke, a yokozuna is counted as ozeki, and is designated as 'yokozuna-ozeki.'

2.5 What is the meaning of the East and West sides?

Originally they were teams; today, it is simply a way of dividing all the names into two.

2.6 Are the East and West sides equal?

No, every rank on the East, from highest to lowest, is considered a step higher than the same rank on the West. So the top man on the banzuke is the East yokozuna, and the no. 2 is the West yokozuna.

2.7 Who decides the rankings?

The committee of Judges (shinpan-in, Unit 7.1), which meets two or three days after a basho ends. They decide how many places a man will rise or fall, and whether he will be on the east or west side.

2.8 How are the banzuke rankings decided?

A man's performance in the previous hon-basho determines whether he rises or falls on the list. Basically, if he makes kachi-koshi, that is, he wins more bouts than he loses, he will at least stay where he is and will probably rise. If he finishes the basho with a make-koshi score (more losses than wins), he will be demoted. If two men at the same rank have equal scores, then their records of the previous basho will be compared and the one with the better record will be placed on the east.

Movement in the crowded lower ranks may be dramatic, twenty or thirty places up or down with a really good or really bad score (out of seven bouts at this level).

2.9 What is the banzuke-hyo? Is it different from the banzuke?

The banzuke-hyo is the written sheet; the banzuke is the actual listing. But the sheet of printed paper is commonly called 'banzuke.'

2.10 What is 'haridashi'?

It is a feature of the banzuke that has not, in fact, been seen since May 1994; but before that it was common for many years. Nowadays the banzuke has a thick black border surrounding the written part; but in former times, if there was an uneven number of yokozuna, ozeki or other title-holders, the odd man out (the lowest) had his name written out at the side in a separate little box. Sometimes there would be both a yokozuna and an ozeki treated in this way, and the banzuke would look quite top-heavy.

2.11 Are only the rikishi's names on the banzuke?

No, all the gyoji are listed in ranking order in the central column; all the toshiyori (elders) are in fat letters at the bottom, judges separate from the rest; below the gyoji in the center are the wakaimono-gashira and the sewanin (Unit 10), and finally the yobidashi, but only those of juryo level and up.

Section 2 RANKING ON THE BANZUKE

2.12 What effect does a man's status on the banzuke have on his life?

Just about everything is affected: his pay, his hairstyle, clothes, footwear, whether or not he has kesho-mawashi, whether or not he has attendants or is an attendant, his food, the class of train he rides in — all depend on his ranking.

1) Hairstyle
Only juryo and up are permitted on formal occasions to wear their hair in the o-icho-mage (gingko-leaf) hairstyle; otherwise, only the simple chon-mage is worn.

2) Yukata and Kimono
Boys in jonokuchi and jonidan wear a cotton yukata in summer, and even in winter they have only a plain unlined woolen kimono. This is intended to harden their bodies — or maybe to encourage them to get promotion so that they can dress more warmly.

3) Coats

Sandanme men may wear a haori, a Japanese-style light jacket, while those in makushita can be comfortable in (Japanese) overcoats and scarfs.

4) Hakama (divided skirt)

This formal Japanese-style garment is permitted only to sekitori, that is, juryo and above.

5) Obi (cloth belt)

Men in the bottom three divisions wear a broad obi of soft crepe, wrapped and tied in a way that is unique to them. Makushita and above wear a rigid weave called hakata ori (from an old part of Fukuoka in Kyushu). A yokozuna's obi is of crepe, but of a firmer kind. All obi, however, are made of silk.

6) Footwear

The two lowest divisions wear geta, thonged wooden clogs raised from the ground on transverse slats; their feet are otherwise bare. From sandanme, they wear setta, comfortable sandals which, like geta, have a thong between the big toe and the other toes. But even here there is a division: the sandanme have to be content with setta made of plastic or possibly leather, whereas from makushita the part of the setta that touches the sole of the foot is made of woven strips of bamboo bark, that looks like soft straw. Nowadays, however, even these are likely to be plastic imitations.

7) Tabi (socks)

These traditional Japanese-style socks, with a separate compartment for the big toes (required to fit into the thongs in Japanese-style footwear), are permitted to men of makushita and above. Those below this level have bare feet. Sekitori wear white tabi, while those below wear black.

8) Keiko-mawashi

For training (keiko), all rikishi wear a firmly-woven cotton mawashi, but those in the bottom four divisions have black mawashi whereas the sekitori wear white. It is a creamy natural color, not a real white.

9) Dohyo-iri

Only juryo and above have a ring-entering ceremony.

10) Shimekomi

Makushita and below have only one mawashi, the black one they wear for training. During basho time, they have their official bouts in it too, since it is the only one they have. Juryo and above have, for public bouts, a silk mawashi called a shimekomi. These days they choose from a wide variety of colors, although the rules, strictly speaking, mandate purple or navy blue.

11) Sagari

For a basho, all rikishi wear a long fringe tucked into the front of their mawashi, but sekitori have one of silk that matches their shimekomi, and it is stiffened; those below the sekitori rank, however, use a cotton sagari that is not stiffened.

12) Kesho-mawashi

Juryo and above have resplendent kesho-mawashi, silk mawashi with ornamental apron-like ends, to wear for their dohyo-iri; those below have no such ceremony and do not need kesho-mawashi. (For the presentation of new recruits in the shinjo shusse hiro, the boys wear kesho-mawashi, but these are borrowed from their seniors; they are not allowed to have their own.)

13) Salary

Once a man becomes a juryo, he begins to receive a regular monthly salary. Non-sekitori are not without income, but they get a basho-teate, an allowance paid every two months. The amount goes up according to rank.

14) Tsukebito

Boys and men in the lowest four divisions are assigned to act as tsukebito (literally 'attached persons') — valets, assistants, servants, what you will — to one of their seniors. A man promoted to the juryo division is usually assigned two tsukebito, and the number rises as his rank goes up. When he announces his retirement he is still left with two tsukebito to help him with the preparations for his retirement ceremony. A stablemaster also has a tsukebito to wait on him, and his selection of such an attendant is usually a mark of favor. When a gyoji is promoted to the juryo level, he is also assigned a tsukebito to carry the heavy box 'akeni' that contains his heavy silk costumes.

15) Private room

On promotion to juryo, a man is assigned a private room; before that, he lives communally, although even here there is a difference: the lower ranks have one big dormitory room, whereas the makushita are often permitted to use the agari-zashiki, the viewing area around the training area, as a living room in the evening and a bedroom at night.

16) Number of bouts in hon-basho

Sekitori have a bout on each of the 15 days, but the bottom four divisions have only seven bouts.

17) Hikae-zabuton

Only men in the makuuchi division are permitted to have their personal cushion to sit on while waiting for their bout in the place (hikae) beside the east or west judge. The cushion is personalized with their name. The Kyokai provides four purple silk cushions for the juryo to sit on. In former times the east zabutons were orange, but now they are all the more serviceable purple. The lower ranks sit on a hard pad of woven straw or, more recently, a very thin cotton cushion has been seen.

18) Akeni

Juryo and up have their own heavy box for their gear. The akeni is made of woven split bamboo, covered with paper and lacquered green, and with the corners reinforced with iron bands. The sekitori's name is painted on in vermilion. The craftsmen apprenticed to akeni-making have already died out, and the Kyokai has pressed into service a Kyoto craftsman who had previously made a similar but lighter clothes box. Perhaps the time is drawing near when this cumbersome relic of old Japan will disappear from the scene. Certainly the youngest of the apprentices, who have to carry the great weight of their senior's akeni on their shoulder, would welcome its disappearance.

19) Bathing order

Although the top division men are the last to train, they are also the first to enter the communal bath. Then the other rikishi use the bath in descending order, ending with the newest recruits.

20) Eating order

As with the bath, so with meals. The highest-ranked men eat first, and the lowest, who were up around dawn, eat last. In the bad old days there was often little left but gravy, but in these more affluent days everybody has a full stomach.

21) Cars

Parking space in the Kokugikan's underground car park is limited, so only yokozuna and ozeki are allowed to drive in and park their cars there. Everybody else has to get out of cars and taxis on the street, and walk in past crowds of gawking fans.

22) Train seats

As you might expect, there are two classes of seats used on the express trains used for traveling to out-of-Tokyo basho and on tour. On the Shinkansen, the so-called Bullet Train, only the makuuchi get first-class seats in the Green Car; even the juryo have to sit in the ordinary cars with the lower ranks.

Section 3 WHAT DO RIKISHI WEAR?

o MAWASHI

2.13 What is a mawashi?

This is the general term for the long strip of firm cloth that is the basic wear of the rikishi.

2.14 What is a mawashi made of?

For keiko (training), it is made of thick, closely-woven cotton that is bought directly from the Kokugikan. Two large drums, one of white and one of black cloth about 80 cm wide, are set on a frame at the end of a corridor. The floor is marked in meters. When a stablemaster sends someone to buy what his heya needs, the length of cloth is pulled out up to the appropriate mark on the floor and cut off.

2.15 Is the color of the cotton mawashi fixed?

Yes, it is. The cotton mawashi worn by sekitori for keiko is bleached cotton, a creamy natural color. That worn by the makushita and below for both keiko and on the dohyo is dyed black. (In amateur sumo, however, only the white mawashi is worn.)

2.16 How long is a mawashi?

It depends on the size of the wearer and how many times he wants it to go round his waist; but in general it varies between 7 and 9 meters. It is folded lengthwise into four, and with one end held against the stomach, passed between the legs (at which point it is folded again to make it narrower), turned at a right angle at the back and lapped around five to seven times, finished in a single-ended knot at the back. (The front end, folded into a triangle for the juniors, has already disappeared under the layers of belt at the front, while the seniors leave the front end hanging loose and tuck it into the top of the belt for keiko.)

2.17 Can a cotton mawashi be washed?

Yes, it can, though this is not done too often, and only water is used, not soap. It is laid along the pavement, water is poured over and it is scrubbed with yard brushes. But every day after keiko all the cotton mawashi are hung out to dry and air in the fresh air and sunshine as much as possible.

2.18 How long does a mawashi last?

About a year.

o SHIMEKOMI

2.19 What is a shimekomi?

It is the silk mawashi worn for tournaments by sekitori. It is also called torimawashi.

2.20 How does it differ from the mawashi above?

Apart from being made of closely woven Kyoto silk satin, it is much the same except that it is folded into six to put on, and these days it is likely to be brightly colored.

2.21 Can men below juryo level wear a shimekomi?

No. Men at makushita level and below have only one mawashi, the black cotton one used for training; they have to wear this on the dohyo too (even if a supporter offered to buy a silk one!).

2.22 Can a sekitori appear for a bout on the dohyo in something other than a shimekomi?

No. It is the rule that they must wear a silk mawashi.

2.23 Is the color of the shimekomi fixed?

Oddly enough, there is still a rule that it must be navy blue or purple; but in fact since the advent of color television many colors are used, and since they add to the spectacle, the Kyokai has never objected. Some men like Asanowaka in his earlier days, seem to revel in wearing the most eye-catching color they can find, whilst others, like Musoyama, prefer sober colors such as gun-metal.

2.24 How long does a shimekomi last?

Usually, about three years if it is properly cared for.

2.25 Can a shimekomi be washed?

No, it must on no account be washed, even though it gets damp and stained with the sekitori's sweat. Nor can it be dry-cleaned, since this softens the rigid silk. Unlike a keiko mawashi, a shimekomi must be aired indoors, out of sunshine.

2.26 Is there any rule for how tight the shimekomi should be wound?

There is no rule as such, though a very loose wrap may make it hard for an opponent to get a firm belt grip. If the looseness appears deliberate, the sekitori may receive a warning from the Kyokai. On the other hand, a very tight wrapping prevents an opponent from getting his fingertips under the belt at all. The only thing to beware of is that if the knot comes loose the whole mawashi may drop off - and this is not only embarrassing but results in a loss by disqualification.

2.27 Do the rikishi wear anything under their mawashi?

They wear nothing under the keiko mawashi or the shimekomi. Under the kesho mawashi, however, they wear a white cotton fundoshi, loincloth, to protect the valuable object that will continue to be a treasured souvenir.

2.28 Can a woman touch a shimekomi?

There is a very strong feeling that she shouldn't. Even during the manufacture, it is customary in the shop and the weaving shed to have all the work on a shimekomi done only by men, even though women play an active part in the silk industry at large.

2.29 When did the shimekomi and the kesho-mawashi become separate garments?

In the Heian period (794-1185), the wrestlers wore a length of soft white cloth called a tousagi. It was put on in much the same way as the mawashi of today, but the front part was a loose loincloth and the back was tied in an elaborate pattern of knots that in the old paintings look something like macrame. The soft material would have given no opportunity for a belt grip, and it is clear that sumo in those days was very different.

As the 18th century turned into the 19th, the pictures show us a dohyo-iri in which the men wore one garment that was a mixture of today's two: a patterned mawashi with a wide fringed end much wider than today's. It was more like a skirt, going almost all the way round to the back, and it came down to the knees. This 'skirt' gradually got shorter, and eventually separated into the shimekomi and the kesho-mawashi.

The kesho mawashi as a special garment used only for the dohyo-iri emerged, according to some authorities, in the mid-18th century, and according to others, at the end of that century.

The fringe on the shimekomi also separated off, into the sagari of modern times.

o SAGARI

2.30 What is a sagari?

Technically, it should be plural. Sagari are the cords hanging from a strip of cloth that is tucked into the belt before the wrapping around is finished, being held in place only by the upper laps of material. The name means simply 'hanging things.'

For convenience we will treat sagari here as a singular noun that refers to the whole item that is an additional part of the mawashi or shimekomi worn on the dohyo.

2.31 Is there a fixed number of strings?

No, but there must be an odd number. This is because it is considered to be related to the twists of straw hanging at the entrances to Shinto shrines, which are always an odd number. A few decades ago it was common to have 17, 19 or even 21 strings, but the number has greatly decreased. Since the 1980s, a sagari of 13 strings is common. But it depends on the individual.

2.32 What is the sagari made of?

Cotton for the makushita and below; for the sekitori it is made from an offcut of the shimekomi, so it is the same color as that.

2.33 Why does the sagari look like knitting needles?

The silk sagari is stiffened; the cotton one is not. A sekitori's chief tsukebito makes two sets of sagari about a week before a basho starts. The 'strings' are bunches of silk floss hanging from the width of silk that has been sent by the weaver. A sheet of dried laver seaweed is boiled until it is soft, then strained through a cloth. While it is boiling, the tsukebito pins the two offcuts to upright boards and separates the floss into the number of strands he wants. Then he covers his hands in the vegetable gum he has made, and forms each strand into a straight needle-like shape. When the two sets of sagari are finished — the work takes about an hour and a half — they are left on the boards to dry out for three days. The final task is to trim off the razor-sharp ends, that once hardened could do real damage both to the silk kesho mawashi and to the rikishi's skin.

2.34 Who makes the sagari for the lower ranks?

They are bought ready-made from a shop in Ryogoku, at a cost of one thousand two hundred yen. There is no limit on color these days (formerly they were all black), and the youngsters choose what they like. The strands are not stiffened, and hang loose.

2.35 Does the sagari come off easily?

Yes, a sagari often comes off in the course of a bout and falls to the dohyo; if possible, the gyoji picks the article up and tosses it to the yobidashi at the corner. This is to prevent it from fouling the feet of the contestants. The gyoji will also try to remove a sagari that is coming loose, for the same reason. At the end of the bout, if necessary, the rikishi removes the sagari and the winner hands his to the yobidashi on the corner. The yobidashi gathers it neatly together until it is the shape of a hammer, and threads the stiffened 'needles' through the binding on any prize money envelopes the man may have won. When the man has offered the Water of Power (4.13), he takes the sagari and leaves.

Section 4 KESHO-MAWASHI

2.36 What is a kesho-mawashi?

It is a decorative form of mawashi worn by sekitori for their dohyo-iri, ring-entering ceremonies. Unlike other forms of mawashi, one end, the maedare, is richly embroidered or otherwise decorated, and is worn hanging down in front like an apron.

2.37 Can a rikishi buy one for himself?

No; kesho-mawashi are always presented, by individuals or groups.

2.38 Can anybody besides sekitori wear a kesho-mawashi?

On certain occasions, juniors may wear borrowed kesho-mawashi, but they may not own them.

1) After passing mae-zumo, the new entrants are presented to the public in the shinjo shusse hiro ceremony (1.18), and on this occasion they are wearing kesho-mawashi borrowed from their seniors.

2) At an informal sumo occasion such as on jungyo or preceding the hair-cutting retirement ceremony, five or six juniors mount the dohyo to sing jinku, sumo-style songs. They, too, wear borrowed kesho-mawashi.

3) The junior rikishi who performs the yumitori-shiki 'bow-twirling ceremony' at the end of the sumo day always wears a kesho-mawashi because he represents the winner of the final bout, who is a sekitori. Strictly speaking, the kesho-mawashi belongs to the Sumo Kyokai but it may be regarded as his, since no-one else wears it.

2.39 Are kesho-mawashi a fixed size?

Not really. The length, which would vary with the girth of the wearer, averages about seven meters. The width is about 80 cm. for all sizes of sekitori, which means that its appearance varies greatly, according to whether the man is large or relatively small.

2.40 How is a kesho-mawashi made?

An order is sent to Kyoto for either hakata ori, a kind of weave that can be made by machine, or the even more expensive nishijin, that must be handwoven. The weaver dyes the necessary amount of silk and sets up his loom. Production of the silk takes from ten to twenty days.

Back in Tokyo, the finished length of silk goes to one of a number of small manufacturers. The last meter of one end, which will become the maedare, the part resembling an apron, is lined with brocade, and the heavy twisted fringe, the baren, is sewn to the bottom. The baren is made elsewhere by a specialist; about 100 fat loops of very fine wire-covered silk are twisted and braided into a double row; in wear, about 40 will be visible at any one time.

The design is sometimes merely painted on the front of the maedare, but more often it is embroidered in so-called satin stitch (long-and-short stitch). The characters of the rikishi's shikona, the name of the donor, and sometimes separate parts of the design intended to stand out from the rest, are embroidered separately and attached later by applique.

The kesho-mawashi is ready five or six weeks after the order was placed. The supporters give a party to celebrate the promotion of their protege, and one or more kesho-mawashi will be on display, hanging down from a wooden frame to show them to best advantage.

2.41 Who gives a kesho-mawashi?

Normally, the heya's koenkai (supporters' association) gives one to celebrate a promotion; when a man is promoted to juryo he is entitled to have his own personal koenkai, too, and they will be proud and happy to oblige. A popular man who belongs to a popular heya may have koenkai in more than one place; his home town, and also Tokyo, for instance. A business firm may also sponsor a rikishi and donate a kesho-mawashi bearing the company logo or at least its name written along the top of the baren. Some of the university sumo clubs also make a point of giving each of their alumni his first kesho-mawashi, and this will be identical in each case. So it is sometimes possible to pick out all the Nihon U. men if they all choose to wear their identical kesho-mawashi on the dohyo together. Occasionally an individual may donate a kesho-mawashi too.

2.42 Who is responsible for the yokozuna's sets of kesho-mawashi?

The yokozuna's supporters have to give him kesho-mawashi in sets of three. The two attendants have to wear the yokozuna's kesho-mawashi, and not their own, in the makuuchi dohyo-iri that precedes the yokozuna dohyo-iri, because there is no time for them to change.

2.43 Is a kesho-mawashi worn in exactly the same way as any other mawashi?

There are small differences. Since a kesho-mawashi is so valuable, a white cotton loincloth, fundoshi, is worn underneath to protect the fabric; the part beyond the maedare is folded lengthwise into six, not four; and the knot at the back does not have to be tied so tightly since it is not subjected to so much strain.

2.44 What is the origin of the kesho-mawashi?

The kesho mawashi as a special garment used only for the dohyo-iri emerged, according to some authorities, in the mid-18th century, and according to others, at the end of that century. The feudal lords, daimyo, liked to have strong sumo wrestlers among their retainers, and so when parading before the audience these men would wear a mawashi bearing a simple design — a stripe, a chevron, a circle — that showed which lord was their master. Those old kesho-mawashi, some of which can still be seen in the Sumo Museum inside the Kokugikan, were very simple and inexpensive. But a class of rich townsmen grew up. To keep them in their place, laws were passed forbidding them to wear expensive clothing; instead, to show their wealth, they began to load their favorite rikishi with increasingly costly silk garments.

UNIT 3 THE KOKUGIKAN

Section 1 KOKUGIKAN inside and outside

3.1 What does the name mean?

Literally, the hall (kan) of the national (koku) art or sport (gi).

3.2 Where is the Kokugikan?

The present Kokugikan is called Ryogoku Kokugikan in conscious imitation of the earliest covered hall but it is actually situated in the Yokoami section north of the train line (Ryogoku proper is to the south).

3.3 When did the Kokugikan open?

It opened in January 1985. In September 1984 the final basho was held in the old Kuramae Kokugikan, which was then demolished and turned into a high-tech sewage treatment plant. By coincidence the old Ryogoku Kokugikan, that had for many years been used, not for sumo but as the hall of Nihon University, was also demolished in 1984, so that September there were three Kokugikans in physical existence: the oldest one in ruins and being carted away; the newest well on the way to completion; and the one at Kuramae featuring its final basho. The old Ryogoku Kokugikan was built on the site of a mass grave made for the 100,000 victims of the Great Meireki Fire of 1657.

3.4 What kinds of seats are there?

The first six rows of ringside seats are individual cushions, and each is normally sold to one person for all 15 days. They are commonly called 'sunakaburi,' that is 'sand-covered' because the occupants are sometimes sprayed with sand stirred up by the feet of the contestants. One row on the east and west side is assigned to the press. Behind these cushions, there are 'boxes' (sajiki or masu-seki) with space for one, two, four or six cushions marked off by metal pipes. In Tokyo, right at the back of the first (ground) floor, there are the so-called 'box-seki,' comfortable and spacious loges with five swivel chairs around a table, with plenty of leg-room. Although they are right at the back, they command a good view, being raised above the heads of the crowd in front. Upstairs in the balcony there are cinema-style chairs affording three degrees of comfort. The Kokugikan in particular, however, is so well designed that there is not a bad seat in the whole place.

3.5 Who can use the royal box (kihinseki 貴賓席)?

Members of the Imperial Family, and visiting royalty, heads of state and prime ministers. It is reached by a private elevator from the entrance hall; before the present Kokugikan was built, even the Emperor had to walk through the upstairs crowd.

3.6 What seats are provided for the sumo people?

Judges, and also those gyoji who wear silk, use purple silk zabuton (cushions), folded over and tied by a cord at the leather-reinforced corners. Although the gyoji below juryo-kaku do not use it, the silk zabuton is placed behind the gyoji's seat between the two judges at the rear ('gyoji-damari ') from the beginning of the day. The cushions for the juryo who sit on either side of the east and west judges waiting their turn are of purple silk. At one time that on the east side used to be orange, but now both are the more practical darker color. For the lower ranks, there are thin pads. The lower-ranked gyoji, who wear cotton outfits, also sit on the same kind of simple pads. Boys trying out in maezumo (preliminary bouts) sit on the floor.

3.7 Where are the changing rooms?

The changing-rooms for the rikishi are called shitaku-beya. They are in the basement at the rear of the present Kokugikan and are 50% larger than those at Kuramae. There is always a separate shitaku-beya for the east and for the west, even when, in venues like Nagoya, only a curtain is hung across to divide a large hall into two.

Along each side there is a raised platform upon which the akeni, boxes of sekitori's gear, are placed in ascending order of rank — the lowest next to the door, the yokozuna in the innermost part. The rikishi sit or lie here waiting their turn, having their hair tidied, and preparing as they see fit.

In the Kokugikan, the judges and the gyoji have spacious tatami rooms in the basement directly under the seats at the rear. They are called simply 'shinpan-beya, gyoji-beya (Judges' room, etc.). The yobidashi have a much smaller room to one side.

3.8 Does the Kokugikan have any other facilities?

Yes; in the present Kokugikan everything is under that one vast roof. The various offices are in a one-story block to the right of the main entrance, and the twenty booths of the Kokugikan Service Association (still known commonly as chaya — tea houses) are to the left. The Sumo Museum is in the main building, to the right of the spacious entrance hall (which is itself sometimes rented out for sales promotions). In the basement there is a large reception room which can be rented for parties and for the retirement hair-cuts of men who do not qualify for a ceremony on the dohyo. In the basement there is also the Sumo Clinic with its staff trained to treat sumo injuries, give health checks, and test new entrants. And finally, there is the archive, and the storage space for the many museum items that are not on display.

The kyoshujo or sumo training school, where new entrants spend the first six months of their career, is built over the road at the rear (1.21). There is also a staff canteen in the basement, where the boys have a separate corner with an extra supply of rice!

The underground car park is limited in space and only yokozuna and ozeki have the privilege of driving straight in and parking.

The Kokugikan was designed to be environmentally-friendly: in the bottom-most basement there is a 1,000 cubic meter water tank filled with the rainwater that drains from the 8,400 square meter roof. The water is used in the toilets and airconditioners. Waste heat, instead of radiating out, is also reused to heat water. There is also a supply of plain bedding and emergency rations, since the Kokugikan is meant to be a refuge for local residents in case of earthquake or fire.

Apart from these facilities, which are out of sight, the regular customer is glad of the various stalls selling food, drink, films and souvenirs and other 'sumo specials.' There is also just one small restaurant for light meals — after all, people go to watch sumo, not to eat!

3.9 How is the electric scoreboard (denkoban) worked?

The original scoring system consisted of wooden tablets hung on hooks. Each man had his name calligraphed on both sides of a thin slat of wood that was stained red on one side and unstained on the other. If he won, the red side was left on view. In May 1958, this primitive system was replaced by an electrical board (denkoban) on the east and west. (In out-of-Tokyo venues the number and the siting varies according to how well the hall can accommodate such large items.) The switches are now manually operated, normally by the sewanin (10-5 ff).

The names of the bouts for the day, reading from right to left, are slotted into panels that will light up at the time of the juryo dohyo-iri. At the extreme left there are some blank spaces for the names of men in the top two divisions who are off with injury or sickness. The names are calligraphed by a gyoji on opaque white plastic before the basho. There are red lights above and below. During the warmup, both upper and lower lights are on, denoting the two men now on the dohyo. As soon as the decision is confirmed, the loser's light goes off but the winner's remains on right to the end of the day, providing a convenient ready-reference.

The denkoban in the present Kokugikan, unlike previous ones, has a space at the right for the kimarite, deciding technique, of the bout just over.

3.10 What do the white banners over the hanging roof mean?

When there is a full house, four white banners descend from the roof, reading 'man'in onrei' - 'Full House, Humble Thanks.' They come down as the judges come in for the start of the makuuchi bouts.

There was a great streak of consecutive full houses that began on Day 11 of the Kyushu basho in 1989, November 22nd. It did not end until early 1998. For the Osaka basho only, there is still a sell-out that started on Day 13 in 1974 and was continuing at least till March 2001 (though tickets for the cheaper seats and standing room were on sale throughout the morning on most days). All those connected with the business side, the catering operators and so on, received a souvenir key holder for the 200th full house in 1988, and a telephone card in 1994. Note, however, that like some of the 'Golden Disks' of old recording stars, the banners do not necessarily signify that all the tickets were sold, or if sold, actually used. (Vocabulary; man'in onrei no taremaku 垂れ幕 , cf. odanmaku, 横断幕 suspended from the ends, as in a street banner.)

3.11 Is the Kokugikan used for other events?

Yes indeed; the modern building was designed as a multipurpose hall. The lowest part including the floor where the dohyo stands can be cleared to make room for sports and theatrical performances, as well as amateur sumo meets.

3.12 How is the shape of the auditorium changed?

Electronically. Most of the time and expense stems from the labor of clearing the cushions and folding up the front seats, which are actually large sheets of plywood. These are folded up double and rolled away on castors. With a hand-held push-button control, the front three tiers of masu-seki are then telescoped under the first static tier (level with the hanamichi opening, with a green 'Exit' light over the doorway). The adjacent staircases, also on castors, are rolled around sideways until they fit flush against the walls, where they can still be used as stairways down to ground level. The square of floor with the dohyo sinks down into a space beneath it, and another sheet of flooring slips across from the rear to take its place, while another identical sheet comes up from the basement to fill the space.

3.13 What kind of events can be held in the Kokugikan?

With its ability to change the shape of its central floor area, the building is suitable for tennis, basketball, volleyball, boxing, pro wrestling, and also for theatrical spectaculars and fashion shows. Once a year, usually in February, it becomes the stage for a rendering of Beethoven's Choral Symphony. The dohyo is sunk into the basement and two full orchestras play on the double floor space, while a choir of 5,000 people, predominantly from the surrounding areas but with guests from as far afield as the US or Australia, occupies half of the auditorium, both upstairs and downstairs.

○ Outside the Kokugikan

3.14 How many entrances are there?

The first, as you come from Ryogoku station, is for the rikishi, oyakata, gyoji, and all the sumo people, Sumo Kyokai employees, and members of the Press. The central entry is for the customers: an entrance on the right, beside the ticket office, is for those who have ordinary tickets, while that on the left is for clients of the chaya. There is also a special entrance at the side for groups. Further along the road, there is a very wide gate. This is normally for commercial vehicles, chaya staff, and for yokozuna and ozeki to drive in and park their cars in the underground car park — a special privilege of their rank.

3.15 Who takes the tickets?

Normally oyakata are assigned to take turns at the kido, or gate. They are in little booths whose roofs are small versions of the big roof of the Kokugikan.

3.16 Are the guards also oyakata?

Not since one basho after the present Kokugikan was opened. The task of crowd control proved too much for retired rikishi, and from that time, a professional guard agency has been employed. These days all audience as well as press have to submit their hand baggage to a search.

3.17 What is the huge metal pipe structure?

It is the yagura, a tower used for young yobidashi to play the drum. It used to be made of long wooden poles tied together with straw rope, built for each basho and then dismantled. The cost of hiring workmen, and the increasing difficulty of obtaining long enough lumber in Japan, eventually led to the erection of this permanent one in Tokyo. A slow elevator is installed inside it, although the yobidashi still have to sit in the open-sided booth at the top to play the big drum. When the weather is windy or rainy, the two young yobidashi do their drumming upstairs under the portico.

3.18 What is the large calligraphed board attached to the yagura?

The ita-banzuke, a large board on which three middle-ranking gyoji write the current banzuke. The triangular top forms the character meaning 'enter,' so the whole thing is a combined announcement and good luck charm to bring in the customers.

3.19 What are all the brightly-colored banners lining the fence?

Nobori, each one bearing the name of a sekitori, a heya or a gyoji and paid for by a supporter or supporters' group. They are hand-crafted by specialist dyers.

3.20 Is there anything else of interest?

Notice the two-tone tiles on the street, arranged in squares that represent the masu-seki seats inside; and the telephone booths with sloping green roofs that echo the great roof of the Kokugikan itself.

Section 2 THE DOHYO

3.21 What does 'dohyo' mean?

Literally, 'earth and straw containers.' Most Japanese written characters have at least two ways of reading, a single-syllable word that comes from old Chinese, and a longer word that is native Japanese. The 'do' part, which can also be read 'tsuchi,' means 'earth' or 'soil,' and the 'hyo', which is also pronounced 'tawara,' originally meant the large woven straw container in which rice was stored. The word 'dohyo' is used not only for the clay platform but also for the circle marked on the top, so sometimes we say 'on the dohyo' and sometimes, 'in the dohyo.'

3.22 Is the dohyo constructed to specifications?

Yes, it is. The dimensions of the top, the number of tawara, and the area around it, are precisely defined. Only the height of the platform varies according to whether it is a regular tournament or an exhibition. In the latter case it is lower.

3.23 What is the size of the dohyo?

Let's take the square mound first. It consists of about 30 tons of close-packed clay, and each side measures 6.7 meters along the base and 3.7 meters along the top. The height varies from 34-60 centimeters. As it is possible to retract the old dohyo under the floor of the present Kokugikan, about two-thirds of it are reused; only the top ten tons are thrown out and replaced with fresh clay. The circle in which all sumo action must take place has a diameter of 4.55 meters.

3.24 Is that a straw rope around the circle?

No; all the straw you can see is in the form of long narrow containers that are fitted close together so that they look like a continuous rope.

3.25 What are the straw containers like?

Let's call them tawara, which really means 'rice bales.' In the Edo period and even earlier, the ring was marked by simply taking the straw bags the rice had come in, filling them with dirt, and standing them in a rough circle or, sometimes, square. These tawara were very large, awkward to step over and dangerous to fall over, so quite soon the ring-makers began to have smaller tawara made for the purpose. To prevent them from being kicked out of place, the custom developed of half-submerging them in a shallow trench.

3.26 All about tawara

1) Who makes the straw bales?

For all the hon-basho starting with the 1961 Kyushu basho, the tawara were made by one craftsman, Miyazaki Yoshinosuke (born Jan 10, 1909, coincidentally only five months before the first Ryogoku Kokugikan opened), who lived in Yoshikawa town, Saitama prefecture, near Tokyo. When he died on Day 1 of the aki basho, 1997, he had been making the tawara for thirty years. His son had been helping him for three years prior to his death, but Mr. Miyazaki's meticulous crsaftsmanship is hard to equal. In addition, it isn't a full-time job so the son combines it with farming. The Sumo Kyokai needs to come up with some new ideas; the plastic dohyo of the amateurs may be in sight!

2) Are all the bales the same?

No; their shapes differ slightly according to where they are going to fit. These are the kinds and the numbers of each kind (the word tawara changes to -dawara when attached to the word in front):

purpose	name	number	length	diameter
circle	shobu-dawara	16	80 cm.	10 cm.
advantage bales	toku-dawara	4	66 cm.	10 cm.
outer square	kaku-dawara	28	63 cm.	10 cm.
cross-corner	age-dawara	4	57 cm.	10 cm.
bucket supports	mizu-oke-dawara	4 (in pairs)		
steps	fumi-dawara	10	57 cm.	10 cm.
				Total 66

3.27 The circle is made of 20 bales, and because going out of the circle decides the winner and loser, they are collectively called shobu-dawara, win/loss bales (or 'bout' bales). But in the middle of each side of the square one bale is set further out, leaving a gap in the circle. It is said that when sumo was outdoors these four bales were set out of alignment to allow rain-water to drain out of the circle. Be that as it may, they allow a hard-pressed man to take an extra step before he goes out of the ring, so they get the name tokudawara 徳俵—'advantage' or 'privilege' bales.

3.28 The square surface of the dohyo is marked with 28 straight tawara, seven a side, with a shorter one placed across each corner to fill the gap. These are the last to go in, and their length is unspecified.

3.29 The steps are reinforced with tawara where the men stepping up to and down from the dohyo put their feet. These are: the middle of the east and west sides (used by rikishi to step up, and by the east and west judges when a monoii (Unit 4) is called); three at the rear (the side ones for the use of the yobidashi who call on alternate days from left or right, and for the two judges in case of a monoii; and the central one for the gyoji); and a single, central one at the front, for the shomen judge to get up for a monoii.

Note: ordinary footwear is never used on the dohyo or the steps. The yobidashi have rubber-soled cloth boots called jika-tabi (9.27); the rikishi, of course, are barefoot, as are the lower-ranked gyoji; gyoji of juryo-kaku and makuuchi-kaku wear white cloth socks, tabi; and gyoji of sanyaku-kaku and above wear light sandals, zori. The judges also have sandals placed beside their seats for this purpose, and these are different from their personal sandals worn for walking in and removed when they sit down. When male members of the public get up on the dohyo at a hair-cutting ceremony (Unit 14), they are provided with light slippers.

3.30 The water buckets used for the bouts of juryo level and up are kept on triangular ledges cut out of the rear corners of the dohyo. The buckets rest on two tawara tied together.

3.31 Must tawara always be used for a dohyo?

For public performances, yes. But in a sumo-beya, for example, and especially in temporary quarters, it is not essential to use tawara, and the master may choose to economize.

3.32 What do tawara contain?

The same kind of earth used for the dohyo, mixed with gravel and sand. They are then tied tightly with straw rope and tapped into shape with an empty beer bottle, which has just the right amount of 'give.'

3.33 Has the official dohyo changed in this century?

Until January 1931 there was a double circle of tawara. The outer one was more or less where the single ring of today is; but there was also an inner circle with its own toku-dawara. The space between the two circles was swept before each bout, to show telltale footmarks, just as today there is the janome no suna, a clean-swept ring of sand outside the single circle.

The sumo bouts of those early years of the century took place in a circle of only 3.94 m. in diameter. This was apparently too limiting, however, and the inner circle was removed in 1931. The only change in the diameter of the ring came immediately after World War II, when the American Occupation forces wanted it to be made a little larger (4.8m), to make the bouts last longer; soon, however, the sacred circle was quietly restored to the present 4.55 m.

There is some talk in these final years of the 20th century, however, of enlarging the ring to take into account the great increase in average size of the top-division rikishi.

3.34 What exactly is the janome no suna?

Suna is 'sand,' and janome is literally 'snake's eye.' This name is given to the wide concentric circles painted on an oiled paper umbrella. (This kind of traditional umbrella is used only by sekitori, so the newly-promoted juryo is likely to receive one as a congratulatory gift.)

Seen from above, the two circles of tawara and the ring of sand between them looked like this umbrella decoration. Now there is only one circle of straw bales and a ring of swept sand outside it, but the name has stuck.

3.35 When is the dohyo made?

The yobidashi do the work in the week before the start of a basho. If possible, because the dohyo has religious aspects, the work starts on a Taian day, that is, the most auspicious of the cycle of days in the Chinese calendar that is still used in Japan, at least for weddings and other ceremonies.

3.36 What equipment is used?

No machinery is used at all. Once the trucks of earth have arrived, everything is done by the yobidashi using the simplest of tools:

tako: two-man and four-man rammer — basically a heavy weight with two or four long vertical handles

tataki: beater — a flat weighted box with a long handle coming out at an angle

kaki: the dictionary tells us it's a rake, but the kaki used on the dohyo is a flat wooden scraper.

kuwa: long- and short-handled mattocks; the small ones, to dig the narrow trenches for the tawara

tsukibo: a short pole for ramming earth in specific areas

sukoppu: shovels, both square- and round-ended wheelbarrows, empty beer bottles, gauges etc.

3.37 Making the dohyo

The following description is based on what happens in the Kokugikan, sumo's permanent home in Tokyo, but the process is basically the same anywhere. It takes three days.

Preparation: In Tokyo, the remains of the old dohyo are brought to ground level. About the top third of the old dohyo is removed and fresh earth is brought in and shoveled well together. The loose mass is left overnight to 'breathe.'

Day 1: Lengths of string are tied at specific points on the rails of the box seats nearest the dohyo and stretched across to give the height and line of the base, top, and corners of the dohyo. Two more lengths of string at right angles mark the center of the dohyo.

The earth is moved into place and each layer is rammed down until it is firmly packed. Then more earth is wheeled in and tipped on top, and the process is repeated, keeping the gradually rising platform within the limits defined by the tightly-stretched string.

When the platform is ready, a yobidashi drives a nail into the exact center, attaches a length of string to it that is exactly the radius of the dohyo circle, and shuffling backwards marks out the circle with the hand that is holding the other end of the string. Finally a trench just the right size to take the tawara of the circle is dug with a short-handled mattock.

Day 2: Tawara (see earlier in this unit) are fitted into the circular trench and wedged into place with beer bottles on the outer side. Height is checked with a simple gauge, and then more earth is rammed in along the length with the tsukibo.

When the circle is complete, they start on the outer square. The trench is dug, and tawara are fitted in from the center of a side, that is, right behind the toku-dawara of the circle. The cross-corner tawara are the last to be put in place.

Day 3: The remaining tawara, needing extra care because they have to take a lot of weight, are put in place: the steps and the bucket supports at the corners. A neat square hole is dug in the exact center, to take the sacred objects that will be put in there at the dohyo matsuri.

The hanging roof, yakata or tsuri-yane, is lowered on its cables to just above the new dohyo, and the purple curtain of the Sumo Kyokai, mizuhiki-maku, is attached all around its base, and finally, the four giant tassels, with strips of folded white paper attached, are hooked onto the corners. The folded paper, gohei, is the same Shinto symbol that is worn by the yokozuna on his twisted white belt.

3.38 How does the out-of-Tokyo dohyo differ?

For the hon-basho in Osaka, Nagoya and Fukuoka, the only difference is that the whole dohyo must be made from fresh clay because there is no chance to use any of the old one. About eight loads are brought in by 4-ton trucks.

For jungyo and overseas tours, a lower dohyo is often made, and the bottom level is not solid earth but empty boxes. First wooden boxes were tried, then plastic beer crates (surprisingly strong), and more recently, it has been found possible to use styrofoam boxes, the sort used for keeping fresh foods such as fish insulated. Once the fish have been eaten, the boxes may be thrown away as valueless; so in finding another use for them, the yobidashi are continuing an old habit, for the original dohyo was created from empty rice containers. The boxes save about one-third of the amount of earth needed.

The boxes are placed on the site of the dohyo, then covered with a vinyl sheet. The clay is then carted into place and rammed down as usual, using local labor supervised by yobidashi. The process takes about three hours. When the platform is ready, ten yobidashi do the fitting of tawara and other things, which takes another three and a half hours.

3.39 Who makes the dohyo overseas?

Experienced yobidashi oversee the process, but local labor is used. Most important is finding the right kind of earth, which is usually done by sending two senior oyakata over in advance to test samples. The testing is very simple: they take a handful of earth and squeeze it, to see how well it holds together. Clay that is used for tennis courts is a good kind.

3.40 Keikoba: The training ring in a sumo-beya

The keikoba differs from the tournament dohyo only in that it is all at ground level, with no platform. It is renewed before every basho, when the old dirty, salty earth is removed and one or two truckloads of fresh earth are brought in. The yobidashi, not only of that heya but of the ichimon, are in charge of making it, but they are likely to take advantage of the junior apprentices as free labor. Since there is less earth, only the two-man tako (rammers) are used. The tawara are less painstakingly made, or may be omitted altogether, as an economy measure. Everything else is just the same.

3.41 Uzume-mono/Shizume-mono: the pacifiers

Every dohyo and keikoba has, buried in its center, a set of objects put there during the dohyo-matsuri. These are:

konbu: kelp (a kind of seaweed)
surume: dried cuttlefish
kachiguri: fried chestnuts
kayanomi: toreya nuts
o-kome: uncooked rice

shio: salt

o-miki: sake that has been blessed

all of which together represent the riches of sea and mountain. In some cases the name has a punning luck charm, as in kachi-guri, in which the 'kachi' sounds like the word for 'victory.'

3.42 Who buries the uzume-mono?

The gyoji who is conducting the dohyo-matsuri (Unit 8). When the ceremony is over, a yobidashi comes with a bucket of earth and a tsuki-bo and rams earth into the square hole until it cannot be distinguished from the rest of the surface.

3.43 Is it possible to have a dohyo without a dohyo-matsuri?

No; even when a new keikoba is being inaugurated, the senior gyoji belonging to the heya or a related one will conduct a simplified form of the consecration ceremony. This is not so much a matter of rules but of deeply-engrained belief that the dohyo needs all the blessing it can get, to keep away bad luck and serious injuries.

3.44 How is the dohyo maintained?

During hon-basho, yobidashi with about two years' experience remove the plastic sheet from the dohyo about an hour and a half before the start of the day's bouts. They sweep up and carry away the old sand (if this was not done at the end of the day before), and bring in a bag or so of fresh sand — about 12 kg. — and spread it evenly over the ring surface. Sand is important: too much, and the rikishi slip and hurt themselves; too little, and they stick and hurt themselves. The correct amount of sand enables them to move smoothly without losing contact with the surface.

At each change of judges' shifts, yobidashi of several years' experience get up and sweep. One walks around with a watering-can, dribbling a little water evenly over the surface, while all the others distribute the sand and the water with their besom-type brooms. The right amount of water is important: too much, and the rikishi skid; too little, and the surface breaks up.

Young yobidashi are also supposed to be looking out for fallen bandages and remove such obstacles at the next opportunity; occasionally a judge will call a yobidashi to remove a piece of debris.

3.45 Where does the earth come from?

For the Tokyo basho, earth is now brought from near Imbanuma 印旛沼 , Chiba prefecture, or from the foot (fumoto 麓) of Mt. Tsukuba 筑波山. Formerly, Arakida clay from Chiba was used, but the supply ran out. For the Osaka basho, they take clay from near Ikomayama 生駒山, in Nara prefecture. The Nagoya dohyo is made with clay from Tokoname City 常滑市 , a seaside city due south of Nagoya. In Fukuoka, they can get suitable earth in the south of the city at Aburayama 油山 and other nearby places.

Section 3 TSURI-YANE — The hanging roof

3.46 Why is there a hanging roof over the dohyo?

Basically, because it is possible to hang one. The dohyo has generally had some sort of canopy over it, partly to protect it from the elements and partly, it seems, to represent heaven above, just as the dohyo itself represents the earth below. Even now that sumo takes place in a covered hall where there is no danger of snow or rain falling on the contestants, there is still a roof over the dohyo. But historically there has been a great variety in the roof or other covering.

In Edo times the roof, yane or yakata ('roof shape') was supported by four massive posts, shihon-bashira, set into the corners of the dohyo mound. In 1909, when Tokyo sumo moved into a covered hall, the first Ryogoku Kokugikan, there was no need for posts or roof, but tradition dies hard.

3.47 Why were the posts removed?

The big fat wooden pillars obstructed the view of the customers in some of the best ringside seats. Even worse, the judges were sitting up on the dohyo, each one leaning comfortably with his back against one of the posts — and his massive back blocked the view even more than the pillar itself. The first solution was to move the judges down off the dohyo, and this was done in May 1930.

But think: if the judges stayed in the same places, their view would now be blocked by the same wooden posts. So the judges were moved from the corners into their present positions in the middle of each side.

This annoyed fewer spectators, but eventually the common-sense solution was applied: take away the four posts altogether and hang the false roof from the real roof by steel cables. This was finally done in September 1952, in the Kokugikan at Kuramae, a mile north of the Ryogoku building and on the old Tokyo side of the Sumida River.

3.48 Does any trace of the posts remain?

Yes, they are represented by the four giant tassels that hang down inside the corners of the yakata. Each tassel is 2.10 meters long and weighs 18 kg.; each twist is 10 cm. thick. They were originally hung exactly 2 meters above the dohyo, but when an exceptionally tall rikishi called Ouchiyama brushed his head against a tassel, they were raised to their present clearance of 2.2 meters.

3.49 What is the meaning of the tassels' colors?

The most obvious meaning is the four seasons: green for spring, red for summer, white for autumn and black for winter. They also represent the compass points and four mythical beings.

tassel color	season	direction	divinity
green	spring	east	Seiryu (green dragon)
red	summer	south	Suzaku (a mythical red bird)
white	autumn (fall)	west	Byakko (white Tiger)
black	winter	north	Genbu (a black water spirit)

Genbu looks like a turtle with a snake coiled around it.

Each tassel also has attached to it gohei, a Shinto symbol. It is a strip of white paper, cut and folded into a zigzag that looks like a flash of lightning.

3.50 Did the original posts always have these colors?

No; the four colors of the seasons date from the 1858 spring tournament. Before that the posts were wrapped in red cloth, at least in the Edo sumo; in Osaka sumo, as far as we can tell from the old woodblock prints, we sometimes see red-and-white stripes, like a barber's pole.

3.51 How are the directions decided?

By the position of the front, or shomen, of the dohyo. This goes back to the Chinese custom, later imported to Japan, of the Emperor's seat being in the north and facing south; therefore the east would be on his left hand and the west on his right. The 'directions' of the dohyo have no relation to real compass points. In the case of the Kuramae Kokugikan (in use September 1954- September 1984), the directions were actually reversed; the shomen was at the south facing north, so the east side was really west and vice versa.

Once the 'directions' of the dohyo are fixed, so are the positions of the judges and waiting rikishi and gyoji: the next two rikishi waiting their turn sit on either side of the east and west judges, while the next gyoji sits between the two judges at the rear. These seats for waiting in are called hikae.

3.52 What is the purple curtain for?

Called the mizuhiki-maku, it is said to represent the sun's journey around the sky and through the four seasons — another indication that the yakata represents the sky. (Maku is a curtain, while mizuhiki simply refers to its rather primitive way of hanging, with loops that are threaded on a cord.)

The yobidashi who assemble the yakata always put up the curtain in the same order: beginning with the black corner (for winter), they go through spring, summer, autumn and winter. This is the old Chinese order of the seasons. As they thread the cord through the loops, they catch up the central part of each side and attach a smaller tassel of the same color as the corner they have just passed. This little tassel is called agemaki.

Incidentally, the purple curtain with the cherry blossom crest belongs to the Nihon

Sumo Kyokai. When another organization is hiring the venue, it must provide a different one. That of the (amateur) Sumo Federation is sky-blue.

3.53 Does the roof have any religious connection?

Yes, but the present connection does not go all that far back. Photographs taken in the old Kokugikan show that there were several yakata used, in particular a gabled one, in a style called irimoya. This can be seen in traditional farmhouses and some Buddhist temples. It was not until 1931 that the present style was introduced. This massive roof, in the Shinmei style, is based on the roof of the Outer Shrine of Ise, in Mie prefecture. So the changing styles of the yakata reflect a move toward a Shinto connection and in particular with the Grand Shrines of Ise, which are associated with the Emperor and his family.

3.54 Do 'yakata' and 'tsuri-yane' mean the same thing?

Nowadays they are interchangeable; but tsuri-yane is the modern hanging roof, going back only to 1952. Yakata, however, can refer to any kind of roof over the dohyo, whether suspended or supported on posts.

3.55 How heavy is the tsuri-yane?

The permanent one in the Kokugikan weighs some 6 tons all together. It is suspended on two cables of twisted wire, each of which can support a weight of 30 tons. In a country prone to earthquakes this apparent excess of quality is wise. Back in the 1970s, in the Kuramae Kokugikan, a strong tremor set the yane moving around in ever-increasing circles until the edge of it was above the front seats. Fortunately it was early in the day when there were few spectators; but one imagines that the judges sitting under all those tons of rotating tsuri-yane were grateful for the strength of the cables.

The yakata used in other venues are all lighter, and of the knock-down type. It takes about two days to assemble them. The work is done about ten days before a basho.

3.56 How is a knock-down yakata assembled?

First, the aluminum frame is laid on the dohyo and the two sloping sides of the roof (kayabuki 'imitation thatch') are fitted into place. They are held down by the iraka-oi, a heavy-looking beam that goes the whole length of the roof. In fact it is hollow. It has slots at each end to take the chigi, the planks that stick up at an angle, and hollows into which are fitted the katsuo-gi, the logs that rest across the top of the roof. These last get their name from their supposed resemblance to the massive bodies of tunny-fish lined up at the auctioneer's. The chigi are cut off vertically, in imitation of the Outer Shrine (geku) of Ise. The more prestigious Inner Shrine (naiku) has chigi that are cut off horizontally — the only difference in style.

Finally a big board is slotted into place inside as a sort of ceiling. The modern roof also has banks of lights, a microphone, and at times a small TV camera to give an unusual overhead view. There are about 70 lights, of the tungsten type, so daylight film is needed for photography. At the beginning of the sumo day only about one-third of the lights are on; the rest are switched on when the first juryo-kaku gyoji steps up on the dohyo.

The last thing before the whole thing is slung on its cables and raised into place is the fitting of the curtain and the four giant tassels.

In the Ryogoku Kokugikan the tsuri-yane is never removed, but when non-sumo events are taking place it can be raised until it nestles just below the rafters, and members of the general public seldom lift their eyes high enough to notice it. For overseas tours usually one of the lighter provincial ones, that used at the Fukuoka basho, for instance, is used and assembled on the spot as just described; but for the Canada Koen, the two-day exhibition held in Vancouver in June 1998, a tsuri-yane was made locally and kept as an exhibition piece — a notable first, and fitting for a country so proud of its forest resources.

It was announced in late 2000 that a portable tsuriyane would no longer be used for jungyo tours, to save money on transportation costs.

UNIT 4 TOURNAMENT TIME

Section 1 HON-BASHO

4.1 What is a hon-basho?

It is one of the six official tournaments in the year. A rikishi's promotion and demotion depend on his results in the hon-basho. 'Basho' basically means 'place,' but it came to mean a sumo tourney. Any sumo meet can be called a 'basho' but only the six big ones are hon-basho — 'real' tournaments.

4.2 Have there always been six?

No, the present system dates only from 1958. In the Edo period, there were only two hon-basho a year, and not always at the same season; a third (aki-basho, the Autumn tournament) was added in 1949, but that year it was held in Osaka in October. The Osaka basho we know today, held in March, was added in 1953; the Kyushu basho, held in November, dates from 1957; and finally the Nagoya basho, held in July, was added in 1958.

4.3 Where and when do they take place?

Three are held in Tokyo, and the other three at different places around Japan:

Hatsu (first)	Tokyo Kokugikan, from the 2nd Sunday in January
	(1st if the year begins on a Monday)
Haru (spring)	Osaka Furitsu Taiikukan, from the 2nd Sunday
Natsu (summer)	Tokyo Kokugikan, from the 2nd Sunday

Nagoya	Nagoya Aichi-ken Taiikukan, from the 1st Sunday
Aki (autumn)	Tokyo Kokugikan, from the 2nd Sunday
Kyushu	Fukuoka Kokusai Sports Center, from the 2nd Sunday

Note: The Sundays given are generally correct but may be moved forward or back by one week.

4.4 Have hon-basho always been 15 days long?

No. They have gradually been getting longer.

Edo period: 10 days, but the makuuchi men did not appear on the final day. So the hon-basho consisted of only 9 days for the most famous men. Since the venues were all outdoor in those days, it meant ten days of fine weather; two or three days of pouring rain would simply postpone to the next day of the basho. (This is why the custom of sending yobidashi round the streets beating drums arose: to let the people know that sumo would actually be held.)

1) 1909: Opening of the Kokugikan — the basho was still ten days long, but all the rikishi, including the makuuchi, appeared on every day. The other difference was that, since it was now in a covered hall, the basho went for ten consecutive days regardless of the weather.

2) 1924: lengthened to 11 days (May)

3) 1937: 13 days (May). It is said that in the late 1920s and early 1930s, there were sometimes eight-day basho as well as 11-day ones.

4) 1939: lengthened to 15 days, as at present (May).

5) 1944 (May) to 1949 (Jan): in the confusion that followed World War II, there was no particular rule. Sumo was held as and when it could be managed. There were basho of seven, ten, eleven, and thirteen days.

6) 1949 (May) - present: 15 days

4.5 Do the ranks below sekitori appear every day?

No. The present system, in which they take part seven times in 15 days, dates from July 1960. In the past there was considerable variation.

4.6 What are the correct names of the basho?

Historically, there is no single way; and you can still find several ways used. The Sumo Kyokai, however, insists that only the name of the month is correct:

Ichigatsu basho	January Tournament
Sangatsu basho	March Tournament
Gogatsu basho	May Tournament
Shichigatsu basho	July Tournament
Kugatsu basho	September Tournament
Juichigatsu basho	November Tournament

But you will hear them called in various other ways:
1) By the name of the venue: Tokyo, Osaka, Nagoya, Fukuoka basho
2) By the name of the season: haru (Spring), natsu (Summer), aki (Autumn) basho (Note: Only these can be used.)
3) (January only): hatsu (First) basho

Section 2 BELOW THE DOHYO

4.7 What is 'hikae'?

It means 'waiting,' and describes the two rikishi who sit on both sides of the judges on east and west, waiting their turn on the dohyo.

4.8 When do the hikae rikishi come in?

Two bouts before their own. As soon as the next two rikishi to fight get up on the dohyo and start their warm-up, leaving one man sitting beside the judge, the next-but-one pair walk in from where they have been waiting in the hanamichi path from the changing rooms and take their places in the seats just vacated.

4.9 How long do they wait in the hanamichi?

The sekitori should be ready at the back of the hanamichi two or three bouts ahead of time. Earlier in the day, when the junior bouts take only two minutes each, there is a steady line-up of ten or more waiting in the east and west hanamichi; occasionally a boy forgets his place and has to be called by the wakaimono-gashira (Unit 10). In the middle ranks it is possible, but rare, for a man to miss his bout.

4.10 Can hikae rikishi choose what they wear?

No; only a shimekomi is acceptable (cotton mawashi for the lower ranks); and a tabi sock, white for sekitori, black for those below; strapping or a bandage is allowed in the case of an injury. Yukata and towels must be taken off and left with a tsukebito before entering the arena. In part these rules are for the dignity of sumo; in part, they are intended to prevent injury to the opponent. So no rings or other jewelry are allowed, and no metal fasteners for the bandages.

4.11 Can a hikae rikishi object to a gyoji's decision?

Yes, he can. He can raise his hand to object, just like any of the judges (shinpan) can, to call a monoii. In practice it is a very rare occurrence. It is the judges' job to be watching the bout closely, but the waiting rikishi should be concentrating on his own upcoming bout, or trying to stare out his opponent on the opposite side of the dohyo. He is therefore unlikely to be watching the current bout attentively. So the right to call a monoii has almost fallen into disuse; nevertheless, it occasionally happens.

4.12 Is the hikae rikishi always waiting for his bout?

No; there is a rule that the judges on the east and west sides must never be left sitting alone, so as the day's bouts draw towards the end, a winner may be warned by the yobidashi to return to his seat. This is called kachi-nokori, remaining winner. For the final bout, it may even happen that the loser of the last-but-one match is the only man available to sit beside the judge, so he becomes a make-nokori, remaining loser. It is an unenviable fate, but one that has become quite common lately.

4.13 When does a hikae rikishi offer the water of power?

The man who has just won a bout remains for a minute or two to offer the water to the next man up. A loser walks straight out, so as not to pass on his bad luck. (This is not so much a rule as a matter of superstition.) So the hikae rikishi on the loser's side gets up and moves to the water bucket to offer a dipper of water and a small square of paper. He then returns to his seat and waits for his own turn to come, in the next bout but one. (For more information, see Unit 4 Section 3, 4.15-

Section 3 WATER, PAPER OF POWER AND SALT

4.14 Can you have professional sumo without water, paper and salt?

No. From the kanjin-zumo — subscription performances — of the Edo period, they have been considered essential — though only for the sekitori. The use of water goes back even to sechie sumo of the Heian period (794-1185).

o CHIKARA-MIZU

4.15 What is the Water of Power?

This is a literal translation of the Japanese 'chikara mizu.' Its purpose is not to refresh, but to purify, and in this sense it is like the trough of pure water set at the gate of shrines for worshipers to rinse their mouths and fingers. It is also called 'kiyome no mizu' (water of purification) and 'keshomizu' (water of adornment). It used to be a custom of the samurai, when nerving themselves for a desperate effort, to take a 'kakugo no mizu-sakazuki' — a sake cup of the 'water of determination.' A shallow sake cup was used for offering chikara mizu in sumo right through from the Edo period until well into this century; the bamboo dipper we see today, similar to the one used in the Tea Ceremony, was introduced in January 1941.

4.16 Who receives the water?

Sekitori, that is, juryo and up. But at the beginning of the juryo bouts, it often happens that a man from the upper ranks of the makushita (makushita joijin) is brought up to fight a juryo, and in this case he is treated as juryo: that is, he receives the water, and throws the salt, as well as being permitted to wear his hair in the gingko-leaf style.

4.17 Can anyone offer the water?

It is normally given to the man on his side, east or west, by the winner before he leaves the auditorium. The loser walks straight out, so as not to pass on his bad luck, and the water is given by the next-but-one contestant, who rises from his cushion to move to the corner. It often happens at the end of the day that there is no-one left on one side to give the water, and in this case two people can do it. Preferably the rikishi's tsukebito comes from the shitaku-beya; if he fails to come in time, the yobidashi can do it. Until quite recently it was customary for the tsukebito to put on his own cotton mawashi, but lately it has been sufficient for him to pull down his yukata, baring his right arm and shoulder, and tuck up one corner of the hem, baring his left leg.

In the case of a play-off for the championship, chikara-mizu does not have to be given, since it is technically outside the hon-basho; but the yobidashi on the corners can give it. If a judges' conference decrees that a match shall be repeated, the water is not given a second time, although the rest of the preliminaries (shikiri-naoshi) are observed.

4.18 Is there a correct way of holding the dipper?

Yes. The handle is held in the right hand, and the right elbow is slightly bent. The left hand, palm down, supports the handle near the dipper with rigid fingers.

4.19 Is there anything special about the water?

No, it comes straight out of a tap into the cedar buckets. But in the hot months, ice is added to make it pleasantly cool.

4.20 Do the rikishi swallow all the water?

No, they are supposed to swallow some but have enough left to spit out into the container set into the dohyo. It is the spitting out of the water that is considered to be the cleansing part.

4.21 Do the rikishi say anything when the water is given?

They can be silent (which is common) or say something simple and obvious, such as 'ganbatte' (Give it all you've got) and 'gotsuan desu' — the special sumo phrase for 'Thank you.' Alternatively the man offering the water may make a loose hissing sound which is a sign of respect.

o CHIKARA-GAMI

4.22 How is the paper of power used?

When the man has taken the water, he receives the paper, folded double, and first holds it over his mouth so that the audience does not see the water he spits out; he then uses it to wipe his mouth, face, and upper body. The meaning is purification, since he also has his own hand towel to mop up sweat.

o SALT

4.23 What is the meaning of the salt?

Purification, and driving away evil forces. Salt is the world's oldest disinfectant and preservative, and there are many beliefs and superstitions associated with it all over the world, not only in Japan.

4.24 Who throws salt?

In principle, sekitori, that is, juryo and up; but on days when the lower division bouts have been short and there have been few or no cases of monoii, it may appear likely that the makushita bouts will end twenty or thirty minutes before the scheduled juryo dohyo-iri. To prevent a long gap with nothing for the spectators to watch, the top ten pairs of makushita may be instructed to throw salt once or twice. This custom was introduced in July 1962. The purpose is simply to lengthen their bouts. In the 1970s and 1980s this used to happen quite often, but in recent years it has been much more common for the makushita bouts to overrun, causing the juryo dohyo-iri to be late.

4.25 Is there a prescribed way of throwing salt?

No. As you can easily see, there are many individual ways, from a huge handful, to a tiny pinch, and from an overarm throw to an almost disdainful flick to the floor. In the case of someone like Mitoizumi, who delighted the crowd by throwing a vast amount of salt, the Kyokai may warn him to restrain himself until the very last throw. This is a measure designed both to save on the amount of salt used, and to prevent too much salt from accumulating on the dohyo and causing men to skid.

4.26 Is it special salt?

No. It is natural sea salt, with the grain a little larger than that sold for table use. One of the daily tasks of the youngest yobidashi, first thing in the morning, is to fill the big wooden boxes that stand in the east and west hanamichi. They scoop the salt from its paper sack onto a large sieve and rub it through into the box. This ensures that there are no dangerous lumps. It is, however, rather hard on the yobidashi's hands.

4.27 How much salt is used during the day?

About 45 kilograms in one day; so during one hon-basho, about 700 kilograms.

UNIT 5 BOUTS

Section 1 SHIKIRI, SEIGEN JIKAN AND TACHIAI
— Warm-up time and jump-off

5.1 What is the name of the warm-up?

The whole process is called shikiri-naoshi. Shikiri refers to coming to the white lines, shikiri-sen, and naoshi means doing something over again. So it is the repeated process of going to corners and returning to crouch down behind the white lines. Men in the bottom four divisions do not go to their corners for salt, so they have a simple shikiri. In juryo and above, the contestants return three or four times to pick up a handful of salt, and return to perform the shikiri again. This repeated shikiri is called shikiri-naoshi.

5.2 What is the order of events for mounting the dohyo?

A yobidashi gets up, walks to center dohyo and calls the two names, east first on odd-numbered days of the basho and west first on even-numbered days. As he finishes, the rikishi stand up, mount the dohyo by way of the center step on their side (niji-guchi), and go to the rear corners where they begin the warm-up.

> Note: The niji-guchi, literally 'letter-2 entrance,' is so called because the two rice-bales, toku-dawara and fumi-dawara, together resemble the Japanese character for 二 (2).

5.3 What are the warm-up rituals and what do they mean?

At the yobidashi's call, the contestants get up from their seats and climb up onto the dohyo using the step in the middle of their own side, east or west, then go immediately to their corner where they perform the shiko (raising each leg in turn high to the side and then bringing it down with a stamp). In the case of juryo and above, they also receive a dipper of water with which they rinse their mouths (chikara-mizu 4.15 ff.) and a square of pure white paper for mopping up (chikara-gami 4.22). While they are doing this, the gyoji, who has been standing waiting at the center rear, now steps forward to mid-circle and calls their names again, pointing to each side in turn with the flat of his fan.

Each man then returns to the middle of his own side, in front of the toku-dawara (3.26) and performs the shikiri proper: Going down into a squat, he stretches both hands low down at each side, palms down, then brings then up in front of his chest and claps loudly (kashiwa-de, oak hands), then rubs his hands together. This movement, called chiri-chozu, hand-washing, dates from the samurai custom of cleaning the hands before battle, using wild grasses where there was no water, and going through the motions where there were not even any grasses. He then brings his hands up to the sides but this time above shoulder level with the palms up and then sharply turns them down in a gesture that proves his hands are empty.

At this point, the contestants below the juryo level advance to the two white lines and prepare to start the bout. Those of sekitori level return to their corners for the first handful of salt to throw. While they are out of the way, junior yobidashi parade around the ring carrying banners advertising any kensho, money prizes, that may have been put on the bout (16.11). The contestants then throw salt ahead of them and stride back, this time to the white lines in the center of the ring.

First they go down into an upright squat (sonkyo), then rise and go down again, this time into a low crouch, and touch their knuckles to the lines. This is the shikiri proper. This is the time when they try to get a psychological advantage. They are also adjusting their timing, with the gyoji's help.

5.4 What is the meaning of the clapping and stamping?

The loud hand clap is to attract the attention of the divinities. In general, kindly spirits are seen as being above ground or in the sky, and therefore need to be summoned by a clap, whilst hostile spirits are thought to exist in the earth, and should therefore either be frightened into staying there, or else driven away, by heavy stamping.

5.5 What do the water and paper mean?

The water is used to rinse the mouth, not as a drink, so its purpose is to purify. The pure white paper, used to cover the mouth while up to half the water is spat out, and afterwards to wipe the mouth and, if needed, other parts of the body such as the chest and shoulders, is also for purification.

5.6 What is the salt-throwing for?

Shio-maki, salt-throwing, is another purification rite. To the rikishi, however, it has another purpose: salt is the oldest antiseptic known to humankind, so it is hoped to have some counter-effect on any germs that may linger in the loose dirt on the dohyo.

They return to their corners for more salt and repeat the shikiri, until they are told that the time is up.

5. 7 What are the two white lines for?

They are called the shikiri-sen, lines for the shikiri, and they were introduced in January 1928, when a time-limit for the shikiri was instituted (see 5.9 below) with the aim of making the jump-off cleaner by removing the opportunity for the lengthy head-butting that had been common up to then. The rule is that a man cannot put so much as a fingernail over the lines, although he can start from as far back as he chooses. Larger rikishi quite commonly allow themselves more space.

5.8 How are the white lines made?

They are painted by a yobidashi with white enamel, and freshened up at the end of each day of a basho. They are now 90 cm. long (originally 1 meter) and 6 cm. wide. At first they were a mere 60 cm. apart, but from May 1970 the space was increased to the present 70 cm.

5.9 Is there a fixed time for the warm-up to a bout?

In the old days there was no fixed time, and the two rikishi would continue facing off until they both felt ready to begin the bout; but in January 1928 a time limit (seigen jikan) was introduced so that the live radio commentary would finish on time. Since then, the time allowance has been shortened three times. See the table below (the time is in minutes)

	Jan 1928	Jan 1942	Nov 1945	Sept 1950
Makuuchi	10	7	5	4
Juryo	7	5	4	3
below juryo	5	3	3	2

There has been no further change since 1950, so the column on the right still applies.

In practice, it means that makuuchi and sanyaku men go to their corners for salt four times, juryo three times, and of course, below juryo they do not throw salt at all, so that the whole bout including a minimal shikiri takes just two minutes on average.

5.10 When does the time limit start?

From the moment when the yobidashi has finished calling out the names of the two contestants.

5.11 Who is the time-keeper?

One of the two judges sitting at the rear is called tokei-gakari, in charge of the watch. He is the judge sitting aka-busa-shita 'under the red tassel,' that is, nearer the east side. When he sees that the contestants have time for only one more return to their corners for salt, he warns the yobidashi on the corners by raising his right hand in front of him, palm sideways so as to be easily seen. As the rikishi return to their corners, the gyoji glances over his shoulder at the judge and they exchange nods. Until recent years the time-keeping judge did not bother with a watch but merely counted the times the men returned for salt and used his judgment.

5.12 Who tells the rikishi that time is up?

The two yobidashi on the corners rise, offer them their towels, and say clearly, 'Jikan desu' (It's time).

5.13 Must the contestants wait out the full time if they don't want to?

No, they can start as soon as they please, provided that they rise and come together 'in one breath.' If they do this within the time limit, it is called jikan mae — before time. Some rikishi do it more than others; and a jikan-mae start is rare at the first shikiri, but more common at the second or third. But once the rikishi have been told that the time is up, they must start the bout.

5.14 What makes a good tachi-ai?

A good tachi-ai, literally standing-and-meeting, is one where the two contestants jump together at the same time and achieve a good meeting (atari) in mid-ring. The two men must go down into a squat with knees apart, then lean forward and touch both hands to the ground before leaping into action. Naturally there is room for maneuver and even guile — a man wanting to get the jump on his opponent may put only one hand down, wait, then brush a finger of the other hand over the sand with lightning speed.

5.15 What happens if they fail to come together?

If one man rises and the other stays down, or if one man fails to touch both hands to the surface of the ring before jumping off and therefore has an unfair advantage over a man who was not ready, the gyoji or any of the judges can call for a fresh start. This is called matta, literally 'wait.'

5.16 Is there any penalty for a matta?

At present it is hard to say; there have been many attempts in recent years to improve the tachiai. In September 1998, for instance, a new system was introduced under which a man who committed two successive matta automatically forfeited the bout. A distinction was also made between a matta, failing to rise in time, and a bad tachiai. A good tachiai was redefined as either both hands down together, or one hand down, then a swift sweep of the knuckles of the other on the way into a quick attack.

This superseded the system instituted in March 1991, in which a man in juryo rank judged guilty of matta had to pay a fine of ¥50,000, and one of makuuchi and above, ¥100,000. This was decided between the chief judges and the Chairman of the Sumo Kyokai, who met as soon as the day's bouts were over and discussed that day's cases. The offender got a phone call telling him to bring the cash with him the next day. At first both parties were fined, but some obvious cases of injustice caused this rule to be amended from January of the following year, after which either or both men could be fined for a matta. The fine was originally called bakkin, but later changed to seisaikin.

The problem of matta and bad tachiai never seems to go away, however, and doubtless the Kyokai will continue to try new ways of obtaining a better, cleaner start to the bouts. The cause of the problem is mainly the increased height and weight of the rikishi in the top division, which make it difficult, and in some cases close to impossible, for them to get right down without overbalancing.

5.17 What happens if one man entirely fails to start?

It is very rare, but if it happens, the gyoji and the judges are empowered to declare it as a loss. There was one case in June 1791 when in the presence of the shogun two of the most famous men in the history of sumo, Tanikaze and Onogawa, were doing shikiri. There were no shikiri-sen in those days, no time limit for shikiri, and no matta; the contestants merely started, or crouched and butted heads, sometimes for an hour or more before leaping into the tachiai. The gyoji perhaps played a greater part than now with his calls and gunbai signals in helping them to match their breathing and movements. In this case, Onogawa simply failed to move at all and was judged to have lost by ki-make — failure of spirit; while the victory was given to Tanikaze, who had jumped off, and called kiai-gachi — win by meeting the spirit. But this could not happen now, at least in the upper ranks. There is a tale that when Takamiyama (now Azumazeki oyakata) was a powerful young rikishi, one of his opponents turned tail and ran back to the changing room rather than face him; but it appeared that the burly young Hawaiian had brushed him with a finger, so the kimarite was given as 'oshidashi.'

Note: The penalty fine was abolished in 1998. Even now one of the two rikishi sometimes commits matta in the tachiai, but no fine has since then been imposed upon either of the two.

5.18 Can the contestants stop a bout?

No; only the gyoji or a judge can stop a bout once it is in progress; but if one of the rikishi becomes aware that he is injured and unable to go on, he may say so. But the speed of sumo is such that the man is likely to be thrown before he can make his problem known.

Section 2 BOUTS, TIMING AND PROGRAM

5.19 What time do the bouts start during a hon-basho?

It depends on the number of rikishi in the four lower divisions. All of them must have seven bouts in the course of 15 days, and they are spaced out as evenly as possible. The greatest number is in May, when the March intake of school-leavers has come in via maezumo (Unit 1 Section 2); at this time the day's sumo may open as early as 8:10, although this time often includes a few maezumo bouts as well. Later in the year, as the numbers dwindle through boys giving up and only a few entering, starting time may be 8:30 or 8:40. The last three days of a hon-basho are a special case: the start of bouts is much later, 10:30 or even 11:00 or a little later. The reason is that by Day 12 all the lower-rankers have already had six bouts, and will have the seventh on one or other of the last three days.

5.20 What time do the bouts end?

Normally at 6:00 p.m. except that on the final day, senshuraku, they end half an hour early to allow time for the most important parts of the presentations to appear on television. Even the six o'clock finish is a direct result of the broadcasts; right from the pre-TV days of radio, the broadcasting schedule made it necessary for the sumo authorities to tighten up their own time-keeping.

5.21 Are any times in the sumo day fixed?

Yes. As you enter the gate you receive the wari, a page printed with that day's bouts and other information; here, you will find the time of the juryo dohyo-iri given (normally 2:45, 2:50 or 2:55) and the makuuchi and yokozuna dohyo-iri (normally starting at 3:50 or 3:55). The timing is arrived at by counting backwards from the six o'clock ending, to ensure that everything can be fitted in. On the final day, in addition to the early finish to allow for prize-giving, room has to be found for the playoffs in the lower divisions. This happens immediately before the makuuchi dohyo-iri, or very rarely, after it if there is good reason. On the final day in May 2000, for instance, Takamisakari and Wakanosato, each with three losses, were in the running for the juryo championship. Takamisakari was brought up for a bout at the bottom of makuuchi, so the possibility of a play-off existed. Therefore all the playoffs and lower-division presentations had to be postponed until after Takamisakari's bout. (Incidentally he lost.)

5.22 Why isn't the timetable more accurately fixed?

There are so many variables that it would be impossible to keep to a strict schedule. A bout may be over in five seconds, or it may take two or three minutes. If there are many of the longer bouts, this could throw the timetable off considerably. Likewise, on some days there are many disputed calls leading to a judges' conference (kyogi), whilst on others there may be none. Such a conference usually takes at least a minute or two, so more than one or two in a shift can again throw the timing out. Since there are some 200 bouts from lowest to highest in the course of a sumo day, however, the timing usually averages out. When it doesn't, there are a few places where minor adjustments can be made: at a change of shift, the next group of judges can come in quickly or delay their entry, and the junior yobidashi can hurry up or spin out their watering and sweeping of the dohyo. The only big space for a schedule adjustment is between the yokozuna dohyo-iri and the start of the makuuchi bouts (nakairi) when, on all days except for the last, a very senior gyoji normally reads out the top-division pairings for the next day (kaobure gonjo 8.52). If things are seriously overrunning, this may be omitted altogether.

5.23 What else is on the wari?

Slotted into the day's schedule of bouts (reading from right to left starting in the top right-hand corner), the wari carries the names of all the gyoji in the places at which they appear, the shifts of judges, and for the juryo and up, the names of the yobidashi doing the calling. It also has a decorative border showing sketches of the main sumo techniques, not to mention the advertising that pays for its production. On the reverse side is a score card, updated each day, showing the results from the yokozuna right down to the top fifty makushita.

5.24 Who tells a rikishi to go out for his bout?

In the case of sekitori, it is the tsukebito's duty to tell him. For lower rankers, they are responsible for getting themselves to the hanamichi entrance four or five bouts before it is their turn. Inside the shitaku-beya (changing rooms) there is a closed-circuit TV (later showing NHK coverage) from which they can see who is currently on the dohyo. Very occasionally it happens that a youngster miscalculates and forfeits his bout because he is not at the dohyo in time when his name is announced.

5.25 Is the order of sitting on the east and west fixed?

Yes. Rikishi who will meet on the dohyo should sit exactly facing each other beside the east and west judges. In the lower divisions, however, it is sometimes observed that opponents sit diagonally opposite.

5.26 Who changes the personalized zabuton of the makuuchi?

The tsukebito brings it to the end of the hanamichi, and the yobidashi on water-bucket duty (mizu-tsuke 9.15) puts it in place.

5.27 Do the waiting rikishi ever say anything?

In general, no. A man who needs to pass in front of the judge to get to his place should murmur an apology, and when presenting the water of power, may utter a conventional encouragement; in very rare cases he may raise an objection to the gyoji's decision. Apart from these cases, he should sit quietly and prepare himself mentally for his upcoming bout.

5.28 How many bouts are there in the average day of hon-basho?

In those divisions that have a fixed number of rikishi, we can say exactly: 20 bouts in makuuchi, 13 bouts in juryo, 30 bouts in makushita, and 48 in sandanme. In the case of jonidan and jonokuchi there are as many bouts as are needed by the numbers. In round figures, 200-plus in total.

> Note: Although the number of makuuchi bouts is given as 20, it has lately been reduced to 18 for timekeeping reasons. This can only be done when several men in makuuchi are off sick or injured. It has commonly been the custom to bring men up from the top juryo ranks one by one to fight at the bottom of makuuchi, thus making up the number of bouts to the usual 20 again; but in 1998 there were a lot of overruns and fewer juryo were brought up.

5.29 What is the naka-iri?

Literally meaning 'middle space,' the naka-iri is the 20-30-minute gap between the end of the juryo bouts and the beginning of those of the makuuchi. So all the top division events are described as 'naka-iri-go' — after the nakairi.

UNIT 6 TECHNIQUES

Section 1 WINNING TECHNIQUES (KIMARITE)

6.1 Sumo bouts seem very simple; how come there are so many techniques?

Sumo *is* very simple: a man loses if he touches down inside the ring or goes out of it, unless his opponent has committed a foul. But the Kyokai likes to define precisely just how a win has been achieved and careful records are kept. They also like to keep track of trends in sumo; for instance, if the top sumo men are getting too heavy, certain fast and skillful techniques become rare.

6.2 How many techniques are there in sumo?

It's a matter of definition. The kimarite, literally deciding techniques, listed by the Sumo Kyokai are actually the names officially announced and recorded as the winning technique after a bout. A number of techniques used in sumo (such as tsuppari, thrusts to the face and upper body with the flat of the hands), are not listed as kimarite, because they are not deciders; neither are the ways of losing, nor the fouls which get a man disqualified.

In Edo times there were a number of lists of shiju hatte — 48 hands (techniques), but while there was general agreement on the very commonest, there was great variation in the minor ones at the end of the lists. So in the middle of the 20th century the Kyokai examined them all, threw out many very rare techniques, and compiled the rest into seventy, which were made official in 1955. In 1960, two ways of losing were added: isami-ashi, accidental step-out; and koshi-kudake, literally collapse of the hips — really an inadvertent sit-down.

6.3 Weren't some new kimarite added recently?

Yes, the Kyokai announced on December 4, 2000, twelve new ways of winning and three new ways of losing, bringing the numbers up to 82 winning techniques and five mistakes, total 87. Some people, especially foreign journalists, treated this as an attempt to liven sumo up; but in fact these were not new techniques; men had been winning or losing by doing these things before, but none of the existing list of 72 covered them. The Kyokai's move was simply an attempt to describe more accurately what was already happening.

6.4 What was different about the new techniques?

One noticeable feature was that eight of them involved the winner getting around the back of his opponent, implying that a faster-moving man could beat a slow one in a number of ways. The late 1990s and the early 2000s had been characterized by the advent of several strong, fast-moving Mongolians like Kyokushuzan and, more recently, Asashoryu, as well as some small Japanese wrestlers like Mainoumi who had to rely on speed and superior technique; the Kyokai spokesman mentioned both of these types as factors in the fresh definitions.

6.5 How are the techniques classified?

Into yori — pushing (with one or both hands on the belt), oshi — thrusting (hands on the body but not on the belt), nage — twists, and kake — trips.

6.6 What are the commonest techniques?

By far, yorikiri, grabbing the belt and pushing out the opponent, is the commonest; followed by oshidashi, a similar move but with the winner thrusting at the body without touching the belt. These two techniques account for the vast majority of wins in the top division. Following them comes hatakikomi, an undignified slap-down in which the winner takes advantage of an unbalanced opponent to pull him down on all fours or on his face (this technique is constantly criticized by the Kyokai). There follow, in order of frequency, a group of techniques that appear regularly, trailed by a large group that are seen perhaps two or three times a year. There remain a handful of techniques at the end of the list which have never been seen in the top division since they were announced in 1955.

Note: Illustrated lists of kimarite are readily available, and will not be included here. On each day of hon-basho, in Japan the Japanese and some English-language papers publish the winning techniques together with the results of the day before; while if you are actually in the auditorium, you will notice that the name of every winner and the winning technique are announced throughout the day, right from the first bout.

6.7 It may not be so easy to find the new ones announced in December 2000. How about listing those?

By all means. A few hyphens have been added to make the words easier to separate.

1) okuri-hikiotoshi — cause opponent to sit down (collapse backwards) by pulling him by the mawashi backwards into oneself
2) ushiro-motare — immobilizing opponent by pinning his elbows from behind, march him out
3) tokkuri-nage — grasping opponent's head in both hands, twist him down
4) kozuma-tori — grasping opponent's ankle, execute hikiage-taoshi
5) okuri-tsuridashi — lifting clear of the ground from behind and swinging forward and out

6) osakate — reaching deep over the opponent's shoulder to grasp the back of his mawashi, execute a nage (throw). It's like a tsukami-nage but as in the case of a harima-nage, the body leans toward the ground.

7) sokubi-otoshi — with the wrist or elbow on the back of the opponent's head or neck, pull him down on all fours (previously classed as 'hatakikomi' slap down; in other words, it's a hatakikomi performed with part of arm to back of head.

8) kotehineri — wrapping up opponent's forearm, execute a hineri (twist) in that direction

9) tsutaezori — throw backwards while immobilizing opponent's arm at the armpit (it looks impossible!)

10) okuri-tsuriotoshi — get behind the opponent and then do tsuriotoshi

11) okuri-gake — get behind the opponent and trip him

12) okuri-nage — get behind the opponent and throw him and the three new ways of losing:

1) tsukite — the hand touches down without any effort on the part of the opponent

2) tsukihiza — the same, but the knee touches the ground

3) fumidashi — accidentally stepping out backward in the course of a bout where there is no momentum left and no contact with the opponent

6.8 What is the most recent league table of frequently-used kimarite?

The techniques officially recorded for all hon-basho wins in the makuuchi division in 2000 are as follows:

Kimarite used in the top division bouts in 2000.
(order of frequency)

Yorikiri	74
Oshidashi	68
Hatakikomi	28
Uwatenage	15
Tsukiotoshi	14
Okuridashi	12
Yoritaoshi	12
Oshitaoshi	11
Hikiotoshi	10
Sukuinage	6
Tsukidashi	4
Kotenage	3
Okuritaoshi	3
Shitatedashinage	3
Shitatenage	3
Sotokomata	2
Uwatedashinage	2
Katasukashi	1
Koshikudake	1
Kubinage	1
Makiotoshi	1
Shitatehineri	1
Uchimuso	1
Kimetaoshi	1

KIMARITE notes: official kimarite list of 70 established by Kyokai in 1955.

On 4/12/2000 the Kyokai announced 15 additional official techniques, the first change since 1955. They are extensions of the existing ones which had proved inadequate to describe some of the techniques used in particular by the fast-moving Mongolians and by the smaller Japanese. There are twelve winning techniques and three more ways of losing, bringing the kimarite from 70 to 82 and the mistakes from two to five, total 87. Introduced by Tokitsukaze Rijicho, the techniques were demonstrated by kyoshujo trainers Takasaki oyakata (M2 Oginohana) and Otake oyakata (J Dairyugawa) and described by Oyama oyakata (M Ohibiki).

Section 2 KINJITE—Forbidden techniques

6.9 How can a man lose a bout by using a foul?

There are eight hansoku, or fouls, otherwise known as kinji-te, forbidden techniques:

1) Striking with the clenched fist, as in boxing

2) Grasping the hair of the head
   (sometimes a man may grasp his opponent's mage without realizing it; but it is still a foul, and he loses the bout)

3) Jabbing or gouging the eyes, pit of the stomach or other vital spot

4) Striking both ears with the hands at the same time
   (Slapping one ear is not a foul)

5) Seizing the vertical front part of the mawashi, or inserting the fingers into the side and pulling

6) Throttling, grasping the neck

7) Kicking or putting the knee into the chest or abdomen

8) Bending one or two fingers backwards

   (bending three or more fingers is not considered dangerous)

Comment: In general, judges may overlook a quick touch of the hair, eyes or other forbidden places, but only if it seems unintentional as well as momentary; but if the touch or move is clear, a foul is called regardless of whether it seemed intentional or not. Note, however, that on Day 7 of the Nagoya basho, 1999, Aogiyama was given the benefit of the doubt by Sadogatake oyakata, although he had quite clearly grabbed and held on to the folded-back rear part of Asanosho's hair after failing to get his hand on the back of the neck in an attempt at hatakikomi; to the surprise of many people, the explanation was that the hair-holding did not affect the result of the bout. Since the effect had been to straighten up Asanosho into position for a push-out, this was also criticized. Later Tokitsukaze, the Rijicho (and Aogiyama's master), told Sadogatake to pay more attention to the rule.

6.10 Is there any special way of treating a foul?

No; a hansoku is a way of losing, and it is treated just like any other: the gyoji calls 'shobu ari' — 'There is a decision' and points his gunbai to the side of the man who did not commit the foul. If the gyoji fails to see it, any of the judges can raise his hand to signal the end of the bout or an objection to the gyoji's decision. In the latter case, the judges may call a monoii (objection, 4.11) and hold a conference (kyogi). But once the decision is made and the gyoji has acclaimed the winner, no appeal can be made later. An infringement of the rules must be dealt with immediately, or not at all.

Note: The gyoji does not need to stop the bout even if he sees the foul. However, the judges can stop the bout or decide the foul after the bout.

6.11 Are fouls common?

No, they are very rare. Apart from learning in their first lessons that sumo is an honorable calling, the rikishi know that there are at all times five judges and a gyoji watching closely for anything amiss! And, since a man is punished instantly by forfeiting the bout, apprentices learn early to avoid such moves. Nearly all cases happen in the heat of the moment, or when a man is caught in the flow of the sumo and cannot avoid the movement. Sometimes in a monoii the judges and the gyoji may discuss whether an infraction was deliberate or accidental; but the offending rikishi is never questioned about it.

6.12 Can a caution be given during a bout?

Yes, the gyoji or a judge may call for a bout to be halted and a warning to be given in the following two cases:

1) While there is an absolute ban on touching the front part of the section of the mawashi that goes over the private parts, pulling on the rear of the same strip of cloth can also be dangerous and a warning may be given if the grip continues.

2) If the knot of a man's mawashi comes loose or starts coming undone, the gyoji must stop the bout and warn the contestants to freeze in their position. The gyoji then adjusts the knot, checks the knot on the other rikishi's mawashi, and starts the bout by slapping both on the mawashi at the same time. Any of the five judges who sees a mawashi coming loose may also call to the gyoji to stop the bout.

UNIT 7 MATCHING AND JUDGING

Section 1 SHINPAN IIN (Judges)

7.1 Who are the men in kimono sitting below the dohyo?

They are retired rikishi who are oyakata (Unit 14). Their number varies according to the status of the event. During a hon-basho there are always five; on jungyo or for the sumo part of a retirement ceremony or charity performance, there may be three or only two. Up to July 1973 the number in hon-basho varied according to the division being judged; two (east and west) for maezumo and jonokuchi; three (adding one at the front) for jonidan to makushita; and four or five for juryo and makuuchi (adding one or two at the rear).

7. 2 How many judges are there altogether?

Twenty regular judges, plus three chief judges, who are senior officials of the Sumo Kyokai and all retired yokozuna. The twenty are divided into four shifts of five men.

7. 3 How are they chosen?

There are five groups of sumo-beya (ichimon or rengo) and each group nominates four judges, that is, one for each of the shifts. So at any one time there is a perfect balance of judges representing the different ichimon.

7.4 Where do they sit?

One in the middle at the front (shomen); one in the middle of each side (east and west — higashi and nishi); and two at the rear (muko-jomen). To distinguish these two, we describe the one nearer the east as 'under the red tassel' — aka-busa-shita — from his position close to the giant red tassel that adorns the rear left corner of the hanging roof (as seen from the front); the rear judge on the right, as seen from the front (and on the TV screen), is 'under the white tassel' — shiro-busa-shita. The judge under the red tassel has a stopwatch and is also called tokei-gakari — 'in charge of the watch' or 'timekeeper.'

7.5 Do the judges always sit in the same places?

No, they rotate each day, according to a fixed schedule. The first shift appears at the beginning of the day and does not appear again on that day. The second, third and fourth shifts follow in turn, until the end of the makushita bouts. Then, after the juryo dohyo-iri, the second shift returns for another judging session, the third returns after the makuuchi dohyo-iri for the first half of the top division bouts, and the fourth comes back for the final bouts of the day — in principle the sanyaku and yokozuna matches.

The following day, the shift that had been the fourth now comes on at the beginning, the first comes on second, and the other shifts move along too. And besides the change of time, each judge in each shift moves round one position anti-clockwise. In the lower divisions, there is no chief judge as such; each man takes a turn at sitting in the front (shomen) seat and delivering decisions on disputed calls, just as a real chief judge would.

To make room for the three chief Jjdges who come to supervise the bouts of juryo and up, one man in rotation drops out. If he was not sitting in the shomen seat, the man who was there moves into the place of the man who has dropped out.

7.6 What do the judges do when they are not judging?

They take it in turns, two at a time, to sit in the Video Room ready to check disputed calls and relay to the chief judge what they see in the slow-motion replays. Otherwise, they may do work for the Kyokai or their heya, or just rest; but theirs is a responsible position and they are expected to be aware of all matters that concern their work.

7.7 What is the job of the judges?

They are there to ensure correct decisions and honest sumo.

1) If there is a bad tachiai, any of the judges may call to stop the bout from proceeding, although in principle this is done by the chief judge.
2) As soon as one of the judges sees one of the contestants do something that loses him the bout, that judge must raise his hand and call to the gyoji.
3) If a judge sees that a contestant's mawashi is coming loose, he must call to the gyoji to halt the proceedings and retie the knot.
4) If any judge objects to the gyoji's decision, he must raise his hand in a clear gesture before the gyoji has acclaimed the winner.
5) Once an objection (mono-ii) has been raised, the judge sitting at the front must call a kyogi (conference), in which all five judges mount the dohyo and, standing in the center of the circle, discuss the disputed decision.

7.8 What happens in a judges' conference?

The chief judge calls upon each of the others in turn, clockwise starting with the east judge, and asks him what he saw. He may call upon the gyoji to explain his decision, but the gyoji may not offer his view unless invited. They then come to a decision, and after they return to their seats the chief judge takes his mobile microphone and announces the decision.

Since March 2003, there is an earphone back-up for every shift except the very first. Two judges from a different shift who are on duty in the video room examine the slow-motion replays of any disputed bout, and one of them tells the chief judge what he can see. You can see the chief judge intently listening through his earphone. He does not, however, give a decision; that is the responsibility of the judges on the dohyo. This was previously done only in the case of the makuuchi bouts, and the TV feed was from NHK. The Kyokai makes its own videotape coverage, however, and this can be used at any time.

Notes:
(1) In 1941, the power of final decision passed from the gyoji to the judges.
(2) From September 1968 the chief judge began to explain the judges' decision after a conference.

7.9 What decisions can be made by the judges?

There are three:
1) gunbai-dori — (according to the fan, that is, the referee was right)
2) sashi-chigai — a wrong decision made by the gyoji
3) dotai, tori-naoshi — both bodies hit the dirt simultaneously, so the only fair thing to do is to repeat the match.

A sashi-chigai is entered on a gyoji's record and if he makes too many he may be held back from promotion. A tori-naoshi is not counted against him.

7.10 Do the judges decide the winning technique (kimarite?)

No; the winner and the winning technique are announced by a gyoji in ordinary dress sitting at a small desk by the west hanamichi. He has a fixed microphone along with a small TV monitor, as well as another gyoji to back him up. His broadcast is called jonai hoso — internal broadcast.

7.11 What happens if the jonai hoso gyoji cannot decide the winning technique?

He can use his white telephone to call upon the kimarite-gakari, an oyakata sitting across on the other side of the arena, a few rows back from the dohyo, who also has a white telephone. The men doing kimarite-gakari are the four oyakata who are trainers in the kyoshujo, sumo training school. Since the school is suspended during hon-basho time, they have nothing else to do. The kimarite —gakari can also call first if he disagrees with the gyoji's announcement. One kimarite-gakari also sits with the two judges in the video room.

7.12 Can an announcement be corrected once it has been made?

A winning technique can be corrected — this correction is called teisei — but the decision about the winner can never be changed once the gyoji has raised his gunbai in acclamation (kachi-nanori 8.29) — even when television replays or photographs clearly show that a mistake was made.

7.13 Are there any jobs a judge may not do?

There seem to be no rules, but it is noticeable that they do not write articles or appear on TV as guest commentators.

7.14 Have there always been judges?

In Heian times there were military officers who combined the present-day roles of gyoji and shinpan. During the 19th century we can see, in the old woodblock prints, retired men sitting at the corners of the dohyo leaning against the four pillars. They were clearly performing the same functions as today's judges — but we can see from their names, and the crests on their kimono, that they were in fact the sponsors or managers of the whole performance; that is, they could hardly be expected to be impartial.

In November 1889 a system identifiable to that of today was set up and the judges were called kensayaku. The name lasted till February 1968, when the present name, shinpan-iin (members of the Judging Committee), was adopted.

Section 2 TORIKUMI HENSEI — Arranging the bouts

7.15 Who arranges the pairings?

The work is done at the torikumi hensei kaigi — the meeting (kaigi) to organize (hensei) the bouts (torikumi). In practice, all the judges work together, along with a few other oyakata, and with some gyoji to keep the records.

At any meeting of the torikumi hensei kaigi, the following will be present:

1) One of the three chief judges (shinpan bucho)
2) Up to 20 of the regular judges (of whom there are 20 altogether)
3) Three kanji, second-echelon members of the Sumo Kyokai, below the directors.

All the above have the authority to join in the discussion of who should be paired against whom on any given day.

The gyoji present do not have any say in the pairings, and are there only to keep a record of the names in pairs as they are decided.

7.16 When are the matches decided?

The pairings for the first two days of a basho are arranged two days before Day 1 that is, on the Friday. The bouts for Day 1 are announced immediately on the Friday, those for Day 2, not until the day before, Day 1. Once the basho has started, torikumi hensei is normally done according to the following schedule:

1) Makuuchi
The group of judges meets at 10 in the morning to decide the top division pairings for the next day. This means that the makuuchi men know even before they have their bouts who they will meet on the next day.

2) Juryo
The meeting for the juryo bouts is not until 4:00 p.m., after the juryo bouts are over for that day.

3) Makushita and below
Since men in the lower four divisions have only seven bouts in 15 days, it is enough for two days' pairings to be made every other day. So the meeting is held at 3.00 p.m. on even-numbered days of the basho; for example, the meeting on Day 2 decides the jonokuchi to makushita bouts for Day 3 and Day 4. In the case of Days 13-15, every man in the lower divisions has only one remaining bout; so all three days' bouts are drawn up at the meeting on Day 12.

7.17 Must a man always fight in the same division?

No; especially if a man in a higher division is off with injury, one or two men at the top of the next division down are taken up and given one or two bouts at that level. The rule is that a lower-ranked man always goes up for his bout; the higher-ranked never goes down to the lower division.

7.18 Are men always matched at roughly the same level?

As a general rule, yes; in the makuuchi division, the yokozuna, ozeki and sanyaku in principle meet only men in the top half of the division, while men at the bottom meet only each other and juryo men brought up for the day. Those in the middle should meet an equal number above and below their rank. But if a low maegashira has an extremely good score at nakabi (Day 8, the midpoint) he will be brought up higher than normal to meet men of better class. This is to avoid a man being in contention for the championship when his score has been achieved only over low-ranked opponents. This maneuver occasionally backfires, as in the aki basho in September 1984, when Konishiki, at maegashira 6 and in only his second basho in the top division, devastated the top men in the second week before being beaten into a 12-3 runner-up score on the final day by ozeki Kotokaze. Meanwhile the lowly maegashira 12 Tagaryu, whose excellent record in the first week was all against low-ranked men, did sufficiently well to end up with 13-2 and an unexpected championship. But this yusho was really a combination of the two men showing unexpectedly good performances.

7.19 How are the seven bouts of makushita and below spread out?

The general rule is that a man may have bouts on two successive days but never three; and he may have no bouts for not more than three days running. An exception to this is that when a man at the top of makushita is taken up to fight against a juryo, it may be his third bout in a row, and it may even raise his total bouts to eight. In rare cases a man may have an eighth bout in his own division; in this case a win is added to his total score but a loss is not.

Note: Up to 1952 makushita men had 15 bouts just like the juryo; the number was reduced to eight in 1953, and to its present seven in 1960.

7.20 Are there any forbidden pairings?

Yes; the present system is called heya-betsu, and under it, men in the same heya do not meet during a hon-basho. It is also a custom, though not a rule, that brothers or cousins should not be set to fight together, even when they are in different heya. There are, for instance, the brothers Kitazakura and Toyozakura, both of whom first gained juryo promotion in 1998. They have never met in a hon-basho, although Kitazakura was in Kitanoumi-beya and Toyozakura was in Tatsutagawa-beya. A play-off for the championship, however, is outside the hon-basho, and brothers may meet. It has already happened in the case of Takanohana and Wakanohana.

7.21 How long has the heya-betsu system been in operation?

From January 1965. From the Edo period to 1931, the tournament was between teams of the East and West. In February 1932 a system called ichimon-betsu came in, under which men in the same ichimon, or group of affiliated heya, did not meet, but anyone else could, regardless of which side of the banzuke he was listed on. The intention was to avoid collusion between friends, of course; but the disadvantage of the system was that some of the best rikishi never met on the dohyo.

In January 1940, sumo temporarily returned to the East-West (tozai) system, switched back to ichimon-betsu in November 1947, and in January 1965 finally came to heya-betsu, which has lasted until the present day.

UNIT 8 GYOJI

Section 1 GYOJI 1 The basics

8.1 Are any qualifications needed to become a gyoji?

Simple ones: a boy who has completed his compulsory education and is not more than 19 years old. But intelligence, self-discipline and patience are also needed. A young gyoji must learn to move quickly yet in predetermined ways; to avoid stepping on the sand circle outside the ring without looking; to remain alert and aware of such things as a mawashi coming undone while keeping his eyes on the contestants' feet; and to apply automatically the many sumo rules while moving fast. In other words, he must be quick-witted as well as physically fit and with good eyesight. Self-discipline is needed because in his free time he needs to study by himself many things about sumo, including hundreds of complex characters and how to write them in the special sumo style called Negishi-ryu (but more commonly just 'sumo-ji', 'sumo letters.' He is also expected to be well-groomed and polite, since from the beginning he will be working on reception desks at parties and weddings.

8.2 How is a gyoji recruited?

The application has to go through a heya. The would-be gyoji is introduced to a stablemaster, who applies to the JSA through the Gyoji Association (gyoji-kai). But he can be accepted only if there is a vacancy in the fixed number of gyoji (normally 45).

8.3 Why aren't gyoji independent from heya?

From 1958 to 1973 there was a separate heya for gyoji, but it failed for lack of financial support. So, although gyoji are really employees of the Sumo Association, they are attached to individual sumo-beya.

8.4 Do gyoji do any work for the heya?

Yes, they are often the book-keepers and record-keepers. They address envelopes in beautiful writing, and take in money and keep accounts at sumo-related parties. It depends on the stablemaster, and the size of the heya, whether a junior gyoji has to serve tea to visitors or even help with the cooking. But in general a young gyoji must learn to keep a distance from the rikishi, since he has authority over them on the dohyo. Therefore menial tasks are assigned to the apprentice rikishi. Senior gyoji are men of considerable importance and may represent the stablemaster in greeting important supporters and visting shrines and temples to make offerings.

8.5 Where do the gyoji eat?

It varies from heya to heya, and also according to whether the gyoji is married. If he is married, he goes home and eats there. If he is still unmarried, he lives and eats in the heya; but the custom varies as to whether he sits and eats with the rikishi, or eats by himself or with other non-rikishi. On tour, it is normal for the Juryo-level gyoji and above to eat with the oyakata — the stablemaster and trainers.

8.6 When does a gyoji become a professional?

For the first three years he is considered an apprentice, but this is nowadays only in a manner of speaking; he will be doing professional work, his name will appear on the banzuke (2.11), and he will receive a modest salary, right from the beginning.

Kimura and Shikimori

8.7 Why do all the gyoji have only two family names? Are they really related?

All gyoji are assigned to one of two 'families': Kimura and Shikimori. Originally, back in the 17th century, there were several real families of sumo officials, but now only the two names are left and there is no family connection at all.

8.8 When is it decided to which 'family' a gyoji will belong? and who decides?

When he enters sumo a new gyoji will be put into one family or the other. It is the Tate-gyoji who does this. Each heya has links with one family or the other, so that will normally be the deciding factor. It occasionally happens, however, that a gyoji is told to switch families. For instance, if a Kimura leaves sumo, a Shikimori may be changed to a Kimura to make up the numbers. Normally there are about twice as many Kimura as Shikimori.

8.9 How can you tell the difference between a Kimura gyoji and a Shikimori?

By the way they hold the gunbai when announcing the contestants at the beginning of a bout. A Kimura has his fingers and thumb facing downwards and the back of his hand facing up; a Shikimori has the fingers and thumb on top. But occasionally you will see an apparent exception to this rule; the gyoji may be following an older tradition. And sometimes a chief gyoji may continue the habit of a lifetime even though his promotion may have put him into the other family.

About Tate-gyoji

8.10 Why do the two top gyoji always have the same names?

This is another old custom. The chief referees, or tate-gyoji , always bear the name Kimura Shonosuke and Shikimori Shonosuke. They are both the top tate-gyoji.

> Note: There are two tategyoji: One is Kimura Shonosuke, and the other, Shikimori Inosuke, but they are equal in rank. However, there is a difference. Kimura Shonosuke referees only the last bout of the day, and Shikimori Inosuke, the two bouts before the last. Another difference is the color of the tassel on their respective gunbai: Kimura Shonosuke's is purple, while Shikimori Inosuke's is purple-and-white. Despite these differences, both are considered chief referees; that is, Kimura Shonosuke is not the chief referee, and Shikimori Inosuke is not the deputy referee.

8.11 What are the differences between Kimura Shonosuke and Shikimori Inosuke?

They are both Chief Gyoji, but they are marked by the different color-coding of the gunbai tassels: Shonosuke has purple, while Inosuke has purple-and-white. They also differ in the number of bouts they referee: Inosuke, like all the other gyoji from juryo-kaku up, takes two bouts, while Shonosuke takes only one, the final bout of the day (musubi no ichiban).

8.12 Can a tate-gyoji become a sumo elder (toshiyori)?

No, although the two chief gyoji are still called 'oyakata' as an honorary title. In former times it was possible, but in 1958 the system was changed. They are also accorded the same treatment, for example, standard of seating in a train, as that received by riji and kanji (the top two classes of elders in the Sumo Kyokai).

o **Gyoji ranks (kaku)**

8.13 Is there is fixed number of gyoji?

Yes. Officially the number is set at 45; but when there is a very large number of sumo entrants (as was the case in May 1993), the Sumo Kyokai may allow a few extra gyoji to be recruited to deal with them. The maximum number at juryo-kaku and above is normally 22.

At the January basho, 2001, the numbers in each rank were:

Tate-gyoji	2	
(Kimura Shonosuke and Shikimori Inosuke)		
Sanyaku-kaku	4	
Makuuchi-kaku	8	
Juryo-kaku	9	
Makushita-kaku	9	
Sandanme-kaku	6	
Jonidan-kaku	4	
Jonokuchi-kaku	2	Total 44

(This was, incidentally, the final basho of the 29th Kimura Shonosuke)

8.14 Who promotes the gyoji?

The Sumo Kyokai, not the gyoji themselves.

8.15 How is promotion decided?

The Kyokai's board of directors (rijikai) meets after the September basho each year to consider gyoji promotions, based on the record kept on each gyoji's performance.

8.16 How is a gyoji's performance assessed?

After each basho, and also after each jungyo (3.38), a committee consisting of the shinpan bucho (one chief and two deputy chief judges) the bucho (chief) of out-of-Tokyo tournaments, the bucho in charge of personal guidance, and the kanji (supervisors) rate the performance of all the gyoji and prepare a report. The report is presented to the next meeting of the Board of Directors, which makes decisions on the ranking of the gyoji. The only exception are the tate-gyoji, who are expected to assess their own performance and decide if they are still performing as the gyoji equivalent of a yokozuna.

8.17 What aspects are considered for promotion?

1) Ability to make correct decisions on the dohyo
2) Posture and deportment on the dohyo
3) Quality and audibility of voice on the dohyo
4) Leadership qualities
5) Conduct in daily life
6) Any other matters relevant to his profession

8.18 Can a gyoji be demoted?

In theory, yes; in practice, no. A gyoji who is having problems related to his work may be suspended; but apart from punishment for misconduct, being held back in the gyoji's slow upward journey is the worst that can normally happen. Too many mistakes may allow a man with less experience to overtake him.

8.19 What can cause a gyoji to miss a promotion?

The number of sashi-chigai is important; that is, times when the judges have overturned a gyoji's decision. A tate gyoji (Kimura Shonosuke or Shikimori Inosuke) is supposed to offer his resignation if he suffers a sashi-chigai at all. Otherwise, those of juryo-kaku and above are allowed four sashi-chigai a year without penalty, while those below that rank can have up to nine. But in cases where the number is between five and ten, consideration is also given to the number of bouts the gyoji has had to referee; a Jonokuchi- or jonidan-kaku gyoji may well have had more than twice as many bouts as one of makushita-kaku, and allowance may be made for this. Promoting or holding back is not a simple matter of arithmetic.

> Note: When a decision by a tate gyoji is overturned by the judges, he does not now hand in a written resignation. Instead, after the last bout of the day, he orally apologizes for his erroneous decision to the Rijicho (chairman of the Sumo Association), accompanied by the head of the shinpanbu (judging committee) and one of the three gyoji supervisers (gyoji kantoku).

8.20 If several gyoji are at the same level, can they all go up a step together?

It depends on how many places are available in the next rank, and other considerations; if not all of them can go up, preference is given to the ablest, regardless of age. So although promotion is usually a matter of a slow rise in the order of seniority, a less able gyoji may mark time in one rank while others pass him into the next higher one.

8.21 Is it possible for the tate-gyoji position to be vacant?

Yes, it is. There have even been cases where the two tategyoji posts (Kimura Shonosuke and Shikimori Inosuke) have both been vacant because the Sumo Kyokai was not satisfied that the next gyoji in line were ready for promotion. (In that case such duties as the yokozuna dohyo-iri are rotated among the sanyaku-kaku gyoji.)

8.22 Who is responsible for training the gyoji?

For those below juryo-kaku, a great many people have some responsibility: the stablemaster, the chief gyoji and, under him, a gyoji committee, are in overall charge. At the same time, the older gyoji in the ichimon, and the kantoku (supervisors) in the gyoji-kai, also help, formally and informally, with the practical aspects of the gyoji's work. But essentially, a gyoji must study for himself. From juryo-kaku up, each man is mainly responsible for his own self-improvement, and it is here that self-discipline acquired decades earlier will show its value.

8.23 Where do the gyoji learn to write the special sumo characters?

They have to start learning as soon as they enter sumo, by getting copies of well-written characters and practising them. About twice a year there is a special calligraphy session held in the gyoji-beya, the big changing room in the Kokugikan, at which the juniors of all levels practise under the watchful eye of expert seniors. They use left-over sumo programs to practise on. Apart from costing nothing, the columns of different sizes act as ready-made guidelines. At other times, they may use old newspapers, for the same reasons.

8.24 When a gyoji reaches juryo status, is it like a rikishi's promotion?

Very like, in the sense that it represents a big step up — in clothing, from cotton to silk; and to a full salary, instead of a modest bimonthly allowance. A juryo-kaku gyoji is also assigned a young rikishi as a tsukebito, to carry his akeni, a heavy box containing his costumes.

> Note: Nowadays, a young rikishi is not assigned as a tsukebito to the gyoji in the hon-basho (six regular tournaments). Instead, a young rikishi only helps to carry the akeni of the gyoji in jungyo, because the akeni is too heavy for the gyoji to carry himself.

8.25 Does further promotion bring further privileges?

Yes; from sanyaku-kaku up, a gyoji is also assigned a young gyoji as a tsukebito, to help him put on his costly clothing, and to carry his gunbai right into the entrance to the hanamichi.

8.26 Is there a retirement age?

Like all members and employees of the JSA (apart from rikishi), gyoji must retire at 65. This limit dates from September 1958. Up to that time, the tate-gyoji could go on for as long as he lived - or as long as he was in good health. Hence the old story that whenever a senior gyoji died, all his juniors cooked seki-han, the rice cooked with red beans that is used only on festive occasions.

8.27 What does a gyoji earn?

1. Salary and Allowance

The answer is quite complicated, as even the basic salary (hon-po) varies within set limits, according to the record, performance and skills of the individual, as determined by the JSA Chairman. But in principle, the salary rates are so low that allowances (teate) are needed to make up a living wage.

These are the salary ranges as of 1997:

Jonokuchi and new entrants	¥14,000 - ¥20,000
Jonidan	¥20,000 - ¥29,000
Sandanme	¥29,000 - ¥42,000
Makushita	¥42,000 - ¥100,000
Juryo	¥100,000 - ¥200,000
Makuuchi	¥360,000 - ¥400,000
Tate-gyoji	¥400,000 - ¥500,000

The allowance (teate) is decided on performance and skills, and also takes into consideration such things as the cost of living. There is so much variation in a gyoji's earnings, as you can see; but here is an example from the very bottom of the scale:

Basic salary	¥14,000
Allowance	¥126,000
Total	¥140,000

Section 2 GYOJI 2 In action

8.28 The gyoji: what does he do?

The gyoji's job is to supervise the preliminaries to a bout, to referee the bout, to decide when it is won and lost, and to announce the winner. After the names of the contestants have been called by a yobidashi (5.2; Unit 9 throughout) and they get up onto the dohyo, the gyoji steps forward and, with his gunbai (8.60) held out horizontally, he points it first to one side and then the other, calling the name of the contestant on that side. (On odd-numbered days he announces the contestant on the east side first; on even-numbered days, the one on the west.)

8.29 How does he signal the end of a bout?

He announces clearly, 'shobu ari' ('There is a decision'), and at the same time points his gunbai to the side of the winner. Why not to the winner himself? Well, it often happens that both men end up together on the same side, or even out of sight below the dohyo. The gesture to the east or west side cannot be mistaken. After this, both rikishi must face one another from their proper sides, and bow to each other. The loser then leaves for the dressing room, while the winner squats to receive the accolade: the gyoji raises his gunbai to face the winner and proclaims his name. The announcement is called kachinanori. In the case of the makuuchi division, there may be money prizes (kensho 5.3) riding on the bout; in this case, the gyoji now hands the envelopes of money over on the back of his gunbai.

8.30 Can a bout end in a draw?

Not now. Up to 1926 this was possible, in what was called a hikiwake or azukari draw. These were opposites. If two contestants were so well-matched that it looked as if they could battle on forever without a decision, a hikiwake was declared. An azukari draw, contrariwise, was declared when both men were so injured or exhausted that they were unable to continue. Both kinds of draw were abolished in October 1926 and the tori-naoshi system has been used ever since; the two contestants start over again from the very beginning of the warm-up. Since that time the Rules of Sumo state that a clear decision must be made. That is why, during the bout, the gyoji tries not to takes his eyes off the all-important feet of the two opponents. Unfortunately he may be unsighted: in the heat of the moment, one rikishi may get between him and the foot that goes out, or the hand that sweeps the sand; there have even have been occasions when a gyoji was knocked flying and could not see the end of the bout. But he must point his gunbai to one side or the other, and he has no time to think about it or to consult anyone else.

8.31 Can a gyoji change his mind?

Yes, provided that he does it immediately; after pointing his gunbai to one side, he may realise that he has made a mistake and at this point he is permitted to switch his gunbai to point to the opposite side. This is called mawashi-uchiwa, literally 'turning fan.'

8.32 Is the gyoji's decision final?

No. Sitting below the dohyo, more or less at eye-level with its surface, there are five judges, all of them retired rikishi and members of the Sumo Kyokai. (Unit 7 shinpan) Any one of these judges may raise his hand to question the gyoji's decision (igi-moshitate, or mono-ii 7.7), and when this happens, the chief judge (the one sitting on the shomen, front, side), must call a conference of the other judges (kyogi 7.7-9.) Any of the four rikishi sitting at the ringside waiting their turn on the dohyo may also raise an objection. This is very rare, but it occasionally happens (4.11). The objection must, however, be made promptly, and once the gyoji acclaims the victor (kachinanori), the decision is final.

8.33 Can the gyoji object to the judges' decision?

No, he cannot. He is not even supposed to speak during the conference unless the chief judge invites him to explain the reasons for his decision — although it is normal for the chief judge to call upon him. After the gyoji has acclaimed the winner, there is no further possibility of changing the decision. Even if a different camera angle reveals that a mistake has been made, the decision remains in the records. In the makuuchi division bouts, the five judges have help from a television replay being watched in a 'video room' by other members of the judges' panel, who relay what they can see to the chief judge via an earphone (7.6, 7.8). Earlier in the day, however, the judges have to rely on their own resources.

Note: The use of the video replay dates from May 1969.

8.34 Preparing for a good start

The gyoji's job is to bring the two contestants together in a fair and honest start. One of sumo's special features is that there is no preliminary skirmishing. The two men must rise from a crouching position and come together at the same time (tachiai 5.14). The gyoji helps them by the slow rhythm of his movements and the changes in his posture as well as by telling them to get into the 'ready' posture: kamaete! and that there is still more time to go: mada-mada! As they go down into the crouch, the gyoji stands tall but with his body twisted slightly to the right, and raises the gunbai upright over his right shoulder. This gives a sign that the contestants still have more time left.

In response to a plague of false starts (matta, 5.15) a few years ago, the gyoji were instructed to remind the men to touch their hands down, since when it has been common for them to add the rather childish, te o tsuite ('Touch down') or te o oroshite ('Put down your hands') immediately before the time for the jump-off.

8.35 False start

If the gyoji's efforts fail and the two men do not come together 'in one breath' as the saying goes, he must stop them by loudly calling matta! — 'Wait!' or 'Stop!' and bringing them back to the crouch again. Any one of the judges sitting below the dohyo may also call a 'matta' although it is usually the chief judge who does so. A gyoji must also call a false start if one of the contestants puts even a fingernail over the edge of the white painted line, although a man may start as far back from it as he wishes. (shikiri-sen 5.7)

8.36 Time's up!

When the time allowed for the preliminaries has elapsed, the gyoji warns the contestants that it is time: Jikan desu! to which he often adds matta nashi — 'No waiting' (or 'No false starts'). He signals with his posture, too: now he spreads his legs wide, leans forward, and raises his gunbai until it is back against his shoulder. The left hand tweaks his costume pants and raises the hem slightly, to clear the left foot.

8.37 During the bout

When the rikishi are in a clinch and not moving, the gyoji moves around them, from time to time calling hakkeyoi — 'Show some spirit!' to encourage them to start some action; when they are moving rapidly, he keeps up a continuous stream of sound, which actually consists of the one word nokotta repeated over and over.

It means literally 'Left over' and lets the rikishi know that they are still inside the ring and therefore still in play.

8.38 The end of the bout

As soon as the gyoji sees a losing move he must announce the end of the bout with shobu ari — 'There is a decision'. The word shobu consists of sho 'win' and bu 'loss,' so literally we have 'There is a win/loss situation.'

8.39 Acclaiming the winner

The winner, having exchanged a courteous bow with the loser, squats in humility as the gyoji calls his name: kachinanori .

8.40 How does the gyoji know when it's time for the bout to begin?

During the preliminaries to each bout, one of the judges, who sits 'under the red tassel' at the rear of the dohyo (shinpan-iin 7.4), has a stop-watch. When he sees that there will be time for the contestants to return only once more to their corners for more salt, he raises his right hand in an unobtrusive gesture to the two young yobidashi sitting at the corners with the salt and water. They will inform the rikishi. (yobidashi 9.8) The gyoji, however, turns and looks over his right shoulder at the time-keeping judge every time the men are going to their corners, and the judge gives him a nod when the time is up.

8.41 Can a gyoji call for a rest during a bout?

No. The mizu-iri, literally 'water interval,' can only be ordered by a judge. The mizu-iri is called when a bout has gone on for about four minutes, the opponents are in a clinch and there seems no prospect of a quick finish. The time-keeping judge alerts the chief judge, who signals to the gyoji. The gyoji then tells the rikishi, mizu iri, 'There's a break for water' and they return to their corners.

8.42 How is the bout resumed after a mizu-iri?

There is one system for the juryo and makuuchi bouts, and another for those in the four lower divisions. In makushita and below, the two men simply withdraw to their respective changing rooms and return after the next two bouts. In the case of the two upper divisions, the men go no further than their corners, where they get down from the dohyo and receive a dipper of water either from the hikae rikishi or from an assistant who comes in from the changing room. While they are doing this, the gyoji remains motionless, his eyes fixed on the place where the contestants' feet had been, trying to retain in his mind the exact image of how they had stood.

When the break is over, the men return to the positions they had held when the bout was stopped. It is the gyoji's task to get them back as close as possible to their original positions, assisted by calls from the judges, who have also tried to remember the scene. These days it is possible to get help from the judges in the Video Room, where the TV may obligingly freeze the frame and superimpose it on the live picture.

When the judges agree that the gyoji has got the men back into position, he restarts the bout by slapping them both together, on the mawashi or the back. To free his hands he slings his gunbai over his shoulder, with the long silk cord in his teeth; as the rikishi spring into action he has to retrieve it by pulling in the cord. Occasionally there is some confusion when a gyoji is trying simultaneously to concentrate on the contestants' feet, to call nokotta-nokotta-nokotta through teeth still tightly clenched on the cord, and get the gunbai back into his right hand.

8.43 When does a gyoji tighten a mawashi?

If the gyoji sees a rikishi's mawashi coming untied in the course of a bout, he can, on his own responsibility, call a halt; a judge may also call up to the gyoji and say 'Mawashi!' This kind of halt, in which the contestants freeze like statues, is called a mawashi matta. Freeing his hands in the same way as in the last paragraph, the gyoji tightens the knot at the rear of the mawashi. After checking the mawashi of the other man and giving it a perfunctory tug (ensuring equal treatment), he starts them by giving both together a slap with his open hands and retrieves his gunbai.

8.44 What happens if a rikishi is injured during a bout ?

If a rikishi appears to be injured in the course of a bout, the gyoji can stop both contestants and consult with the judges. If they decide that the bout cannot be resumed, an announcement is made. If neither rikishi is able to continue, the rare itamiwake draw may be declared.

8.45 Can the gyoji referee standing still? Are the gyoji's movements during a bout restricted in any way?

The rule is that he cannot referee from one place but should move about in relation to the contestants. As far as possible he should use the rear half of the dohyo and also try not to turn his back toward the seats where the Emperor and other important guests sit at the front (shomen). So he moves across from left to right, taking care not to be unsighted by a rikishi or knocked over.

8.46 What happens when the last gyoji of the day has stepped up on the dohyo?

The gyoji who has just finished his turn goes back to sit between the two judges at the rear, a place called the gyoji-damari. As long as sumo is taking place, someone must always be sitting in that seat.

8.47 If the gyoji on the dohyo suffers some accident, who takes his place?

The gyoji sitting in the gyoji-damari (previous paragraph) steps up and takes over.

8.48 What happens when a gyoji's decision has been reversed by the judges?

This is a sashi-chigai (mistaken decision); the gyoji points his gunbai to the side of the (new) winner, and then follows the normal procedure for acclaiming him. But a chief gyoji is supposed to be above mistakes, and if his decision is reversed, he should offer his resignation on the same day. (It is normally refused!) If another high-ranking gyoji makes a bad mistake he may be called in for a talk with the Rijicho. A gyoji who has made several bad mistakes may be suspended for a few days. Further down the scale, a young gyoji who has exceeded his 'allowance' of sashi-chigai may be held back from promotion for a year.

8.49 How many bouts does a gyoji referee?

The number of bouts taken by the gyoji in the bottom division is always the highest, and then the number decreases as the rank rises. In practice all the bouts in a division are totaled and then divided by the number of gyoji available. The number also varies according to the stage of the basho: towards the end there are fewer bouts in the lower divisions, since rikishi in the bottom four divisions have only seven bouts in fifteen days. From juryo-kaku up, each man referees two bouts, right up to the tate-gyoji, who referees only the last bout of the day. (See following table):

| Shonosuke | 1 (final bout only) |
| Inosuke | 2 |

Sanyaku-kaku	2
Makuuchi-kaku	2
Juryo-kaku	2
Makushita-kaku	4-8
Sandanme-kaku	4-9
Jonidan-kaku	5-10
Jonokuchi-kaku	5-10

8.50 Do the gyoji referee bouts of rikishi in the same rank as themselves?

In principle, yes; but because promotion is very slow for them, a gyoji may deserve to be promoted when the number in the higher rank already matches the number of bouts at that level; rather than hold the gyoji back undeservedly, he is promoted but will continue for a while refereeing bouts at this old level. So you will often see the lowest three juryo-kaku gyoji in charge of top makushita bouts, and the lowest makuuchi-kaku ones refereeing top Juryo bouts.

8.51 When does the tate-gyoji NOT come on last?

This is a special case. If one of the contestants in the final bout of the day has withdrawn through injury, and the remaining contestant will win by fusensho (9.23, 11.15), then the tate-gyoji acclaims the winner three bouts before the end. Then the other chief gyoji, Shikimori Inosuke, comes onto the dohyo to referee the two remaining bouts. The reason is a practical one: to avoid the anticlimax of a final bout that doesn't happen.

8.52 Does a gyoji do anything else besides refereeing?

He certainly does. Here are the main jobs:

1) Dohyo-matsuri - Consecrating the dohyo

Before sumo, or even sumo training, can be performed on a dohyo, it must be dedicated in a ceremony called the dohyo-matsuri, or festival of the dohyo. This is performed by three gyoji.

In the morning of the day before a hon-basho begins, the tate-gyoji, assisted by two others, a makuuchi-kaku and a juryo-kaku gyoji, dressed in the robes of Shinto priests, performs the ceremony, which takes 25 to 30 minutes. The two tate-gyoji normally take turns to conduct the ceremony.

The same ceremony is also performed in each heya whenever a new training dohyo has been made. The only difference is that, unless it is the opening of a new building, the chief gyoji is not needed.

2) Dohyo-iri: Ring-entering Ceremony

A gyoji of the appropriate rank must lead in the dohyo-iri of the juryo, makuuchi, and yokozuna. Besides leading the rikishi in and out, the gyoji also squats at the rear and slowly swings the tassel of his gunbai in a circle.

3) Kao-bure gonjo — Announcing the next day's bouts

Between the yokozuna dohyo-iri and the start of the makuuchi bouts, there is normally a gap when nothing else is happening. At this point, a senior gyoji steps up, together with a junior yobidashi. Usually it is one of the two chief gyoji, although one of sanyaku rank can do the job if necessary. He carries, not a gunbai, but a folding fan that must be of excellent quality, and a roll of papers. He unties the string, and spreads the papers onto the open fan. Each page contains the names of two rikishi who will meet the next day. Earlier in the day a junior gyoji has written all these out ready for this event. After intoning the two names, the gyoji holds up the page, facing front, and then passes it down to the yobidashi who is squatting behind him at his left hand. The yobidashi then deftly turns the page so that it can be seen by all sides of the hall in turn, as the gyoji reads the next pairing, in ascending order finishing with the musubi no ichiban.

If the earlier part of the day overran and there is no time, the kao-bure gonjo is omitted; and for obvious reasons if you think about it, it does not take place on senshuraku.

4) Calligraphing the new banzuke

Shortly after the end of a basho the new ranking list is drawn up. As soon as this is done, the gyoji with the highest reputation as a calligrapher goes off to somewhere quiet where he can spend eight to ten days on hand-writing the new banzuke-hyo. Two younger gyoji who assist him have already prepared the large sheet of paper, by drawing guidelines and filling in all the decorative flourishes that are one of its characteristics. There is little space left between the embellishments and the names, as the close-packed banzuke sheet is supposed to represent a close-packed audience.

The gyoji who does this exacting and highly esteemed work is excused from going on jungyo tours - but also misses the enjoyable overseas trips! From 1985 to January 2000 the man responsible was Kimura Yodo, who stopped shortly before being promoted to chief gyoji rank (he ended his career in January 2003 as Kimura Shonosuke XXX <30>). The banzuke has been written since March 2000 by Shikimori Yonokichi.

5) Secretarial work for the JSA

When the new banzuke is drawn up, gyoji are present to record what is decided at each point. Similarly, when the committee of judges (shinpan) meets to decide on the pairings, one gyoji unrolls the long scrolls containing the names in banzuke order, another rolls it up at the other end, while another writes down the names of the paired contestants in a notebook. Needless to say, the writing of the scrolls for this purpose was done by another gyoji before the basho. Another gyoji calligraphs the plastic sheets for the denkoban, the electric scoreboard that shows the two top divisions. Yet another writes a sheet intended for publishing the final results. The juryo and makuuchi are hand-written, while the lower ranks are produced by computer, thus relieving the gyoji of a portion of the work.

6) Announcing names and results

The men doing the announcements in the sumo arena (jonai hoso, inside broadcast) are also gyoji. At the beginning of each bout, the yobidashi calls out the contestants' names, then the gyoji up on the dohyo announces them again in his own way; and finally the 'invisible' gyoji — invisible because in ordinary clothes he cannot be identified as a gyoji — announces more details, including the heya and where the man's birth was registered. When the bout is over, the gyoji on jonai hoso announces the name of the winner and also the winning technique.

7) Record-keeping

Gyoji also maintain the win-loss records as they come in, on the scroll (maki) mentioned in e above. The room where they work is called the wariba.

8) Publicity and arrangements for tours

A gyoji goes along with the oyakata in charge of the tour (jungyo) and handles the correspondence and other secretarial work. For instance, the allotment of hotel rooms to rikishi is planned by him and written in sumo script.

9) Secretarial work for the heya

The gyoji do a lot of work for the heya to which they are attached: addressing envelopes to all members of the supporters' clubs, manning the reception desks, taking money, writing receipts, and keeping the accounts at sumo events: senshuraku parties, retirements, weddings and funerals.

Section 3 GYOJI 3 Costume

8.53 Must gyoji all wear the same costume?

Yes, the gyoji's costume, called isho or shozoku, is fixed: a suit called a hitatare, consisting of a jacket and wide pants, and a lacquered paper hat called an eboshi. This has been the official costume since May 1910, and it is based on the gentleman's hunting costume of the 14th-century Ashikaga period. Previously, gyoji wore the regular formal outfit of a gentleman of the Edo period, called kamishimo (literally, above-and-below): the most striking feature was its stiffened wing-like shoulder-pieces. The eboshi, too, is an addition of this century. Before an edict of the Meiji Restoration in 1871, everyone in sumo including the gyoji had worn the regular hairstyle of the period, shaven at the front and tied in an oiled topknot, mage, that rested on top of the head. When short haircuts for all Japanese males except rikishi became mandatory in 1871, the gyoji added a very small hat of similar kind to the eboshi. Now the mage is seen only in sumo and kabuki.

Gyoji also carry in their right hand, as a sign of their office, a rigid fan called a gunbai uchiwa, or war fan. In the old days, generals used such an object to give signals. In sumo, the name is usually shortened to 'gunbai,' although the gyoji themselves call it, correctly, 'uchiwa.'

8.54 How are the gyoji of different ranks distinguished?

The greatest division is one of material and length of costume. The gyoji of the lowest four divisions wear outfits of cotton, and the pants are drawn up and tied just below the knee, leaving the calves and feet bare.

Those of juryo status and above wear full-length costumes of silk, and tabi (white cotton socks with a separate big toe) on their feet.

Sanyaku level gyoji and above also wear white sandals, called zori, on the dohyo, and as an additional sign of status they have an inro, a traditional lacquered case for medicine and other small objects, hanging from their waist at the right side.

The two chief gyoji, in addition, wear tucked into their waistbands a short sword (kogatana, also called wakizashi, the thing tucked under the arm) as a sign of their status, a custom that is said to date from the Kyoho period (1716-36). They like to tell people that the sword is a symbol that they should commit suicide if they make a wrong decision — but if that were true, there would be a much greater turnover of tate-gyoji.

Otherwise the rank of all gyoji can be recognized at a glance by looking at the color of the rosettes and cords on their costumes, and the tassel and cord attached to the handle of their gunbai. The rosettes are called kikutoji, and are sewn to the costume in certain fixed places: three form a V at the bottom of the collar; two together at the side-seam of the sleeves, just above wrist-level; and two in the center back, between the shoulderblades. There are also eight on the skirt-like pants: four in pairs where the pants divide at the front, and two more at the top of the side seam at mid-thigh level on each leg; There are also cords in the same color, threaded through the wrists and near the bottom of the skirtlike pants. All the gyoji use the drawstrings to tighten their cuffs, but only the juniors need to tighten the pants under the knees; on gyoji of juryo-kaku and above the cords are only for decoration.

Color-coding of kikutoji, cords and tassels:

Tate-gyoji

Kimura Shonosuke	purple
Shikimori Inosuke	purple-and-white
Sanyaku-kaku	vermilion
Makuuchi-kaku	red-and-white
Juryo-kaku	green-and-white
all levels below juryo	green (black is also allowed but seldom seen)

8.55 Do gyoji wear the same outfits all year round?

The gyoji of juryo rank and above have sets of summer and winter costumes. The 'summer' costumes, worn in the May, July and September basho, are of stiff gauze called sha or ro. The 'winter' wear, for the November, January and March basho, is of heavier silk brocade of a weave called nishijin. The summer outfits tend to look paler because they are normally worn over a white under-kimono which shows through the thin gauze. The ranks below juryo wear the same cotton costumes all year round.

8.56 How do the gyoji get their costumes?

Each basho, that is, every two months, they receive a modest clothing allowance from the JSA. As of March 1997, this was:

Tate-gyoji	¥50,000
Sanyaku-kaku	¥40,000
Makuuchi-kaku	¥30,000
Juryo-kaku	¥25,000
Makushita and below	¥20,000

This amount is not nearly enough to buy a costume, so other means have to be found. For an entrant, the JSA gives a sum of money to a senior gyoji in the ichimon, who then gets from the gyoji-kai enough additional money to buy the boy his first modest costume of cotton. For the much greater outlay involved in promotion to juryo-kaku, the heya support organization (koenkai, 2.41) presents him with a silk brocade outfit. The koenkai will do this every time the man receives another promotion.

Another way in which gyoji acquire new costumes is that when a rikishi is promoted to ozeki he (or rather, his koenkai) presents a costume to all the gyoji in his ichimon; and when a man is promoted to yokozuna, he presents a new outfit not only to all the gyoji in his ichimon but also to the two chief gyoji.

A senior gyoji may also present a costume to a junior, especially in the same ichimon.

Finally, a gyoji may simply collect money himself, from his family, friends and supporters, and buy himself an outfit.

Incidentally, in all this talk about 'costumes,' what is presented in the first instance is a bolt of cloth straight from the weaver in Kyoto; afterwards another craftsman has to be paid to sew it together.

Young gyoji in the lowest ranks may have only two or three shozoku; at the other end of the scale, the chief gyoji may well have ten or more, and the cost of each will be in millions of yen.

o **Gyoji-beya**

8.57 Where do the gyoji change their clothes?

In the gyoji-beya, their own dressing room. In the Kokugikan there is a large custom-built dressing room in the basement under the seats at the rear of the hall; but wherever they go the gyoji have a room assigned to them for this purpose. After changing, they should be in the hanamichi two or three bouts before the preceding gyoji is due to step up on the dohyo; and when the seat has been vacated, the next gyoji moves forward and takes his seat unobtrusively during the preliminaries of the bout.

8.58 Do they have help in dressing?

The youngest help one another. From makushita-kaku a gyoji has a younger gyoji assigned as a tsukebito to help him dress. This is unlike the rikishi, who do not get any tsukebito until they reach juryo. The ultimate in service comes when a man reaches sanyaku level: his tsukebito carries his gunbai to the end of the hanamichi and hands it over only when he is about to walk into the hall.

o **Gunbai**

8.59 What does the gyoji carry in his right hand?

The gyoji's symbol of office is the gunbai uchiwa, or war fan; usually shortened to 'gunbai.' Although it has changed in both shape and materials, its name reminds us that the refereeing was originally done by army officers.

As carried by samurai, this so-called fan was made of iron and could bash somebody's head in. Those borne by commanders were a little lighter, as the flat blade was made of lacquered paper or leather. The general used his as an easily-visible extension of his hand, to wave up his troops or point to where the battle was thickest. From there it was a short step to the use of the gyoji's gunbai for introducing the contestants and signaling the winner.

The almost round, lollipop-shaped uchiwa (rigid fan) is still seen today in summer, when advertising models made of paper pasted on plastic frames are presented to participants at Bon dances or other summer events. It is a very ancient shape that came to Japan from China or Korea some 2,500 years ago. The folding type that westerners think of as 'fan-shaped' is a Japanese invention of the 7th century. The military war-fan developed into a fiddle shape, but in the 19th century the gyoji began to revert to the older form and today the oval shape is standard.

8.60 What is the gunbai made of?

Today's gunbai is made of wood, usually keyaki (a kind of elm), though any light-weight, close-grained wood will do. The apprentice gyoji is expected to provide his own, so family or friends will chip in. This starter fan is a very modest object of plain blond wood, and the calligraphy that is its main adornment may well be provided by a senior gyoji. He will, over the next two decades, receive better gunbai, but at the apprentice level they cannot be lacquered or trimmed with silver or gold. In recent years some gyoji, in a quest for individuality, have sought out rare woods that are left unlacquered to show the natural beauty of the grain. There was even a tortoise-shell one once, but in the hot summer it flaked badly.

8.61 Who makes the gunbai?

The modern gunbai is the work of several craftsmen. The basic wooden shape is made by a joiner. It is in two parts: the blade, and a handle that is slotted into grooves in the blade. It is precision work; the fit is exact.

Lacquering is done at this stage on the blade. The gunbai is then passed on to the silversmith who fastens the handle to the blade with little silver rosettes, and adds silver caps at each end of the handle to strengthen and beautify. For the finest, 18 ct. gold may be used instead of silver; it will cost more than all the rest of the gunbai. Finally, an inscription is calligraphed, usually by an influential supporter.

8.62 What is the cord and tassel for?

The gunbai's other adornment is a cord and tassel that signifies the gyoji's rank. It takes the apprentice, whose cord and tassel are green or black, about 20 years to reach juryo rank with its green-and-white cord; at which point he will need a finer gunbai, usually of lacquer and with trimmings of silver.

The cord has a practical purpose, too: when he is tightening the knot of a rikishi's belt, the gyoji slings his gunbai over his shoulder out of the way, and holds the end of the cord in his teeth.

8.63 How is the gunbai used?

Among his earliest lessons the young gyoji learns the traditional ways of holding his gunbai and signaling with it, until it becomes second nature.

He holds it horizontal at chin level when announcing the contestants (nanori no kata); stands sideways with it raised above his right shoulder as the signal for the contestants to go into the preliminaries (kamaete); then crouches facing forward, gunbai back against his shoulder, to signal that it is time to start the bout proper (jikan); and as soon as one contestant loses, the gyoji points his gunbai to the winner's side, east or west (not to the person of the winner, since often both men end up on the same side). Then, as the winner squats before him, the gyoji raises his gunbai and calls the winner's name (kachinanori). If prize money is riding on the bout, the gyoji takes the bundle of kensho envelopes from the young yobidashi on the west corner and presents them to the winner on the flat of the gunbai. Kensho money is permitted only on makuuchi division bouts; for all other divisions the acclamation ends the bout.

8.64 Does a gyoji always carry a gunbai?

No, there are certain occasions when he needs something else. When he is presenting the apprentices who have just passed mae-zumo in the shinjo shusse hiro, he has to borrow a plain white folding fan from a yobidashi. It is suggested that the triangular shape, narrow at the beginning and widening out, is a symbol of increase and good fortune for those who are starting their career on this occasion. At the opposite end of his career, as a tate-gyoji or at least as sanyaku-kaku, he will take a turn at announcing the following day's bouts (kaobure gonjo). For this, he uses a high-quality folding fan on which he rests the calligraphed sheets of the pairings. And for the dohyo-matsuri, the tate-gyoji bears a shaku, a plain wooden billet that nobles of old used to use as a note pad, until the final part of the ceremony when he exchanges it for his gunbai before intoning the main prayer.

8.65 What is written on the gunbai?

There is no fixed form; almost anything that indicates honesty and 20-20 vision is suitable.

One example: Kimura Shonosuke XXVIII had a gunbai inscribed down the right-hand side: 知進知退 chishin chitai (know when to advance and when to retreat) and down the left side: 随時出処 zuiji shussho (The essence, or source, of knowledge).

A gunbai that is sometimes displayed in the Sumo Museum is a great treasure, calligraphed by Konoe Fumimaro when he was Prime Minister (his grandson Hosokawa Morihiro also became Prime Minister in the 1980s). The inscription reads: 至誠如神 shisei joshin (integrity is godlike).

UNIT 9 YOBIDASHI

Section 1 YOBIDASHI 1 The basics

9.1 What qualifications does a yobidashi need?

The same as for a gyoji, a tokoyama or any other JSA employee: to have finished compulsory education and be a male of under 20 years of age; and, naturally, to be in good health. As with the other jobs, the first three years of a yobidashi's work are described as 'minarai,' apprenticeship, but nowadays they receive a modest salary from the beginning.

9.2 How does a boy become a yobidashi?

By being taken on by the master of a sumo-beya. If the master wants a yobidashi in his heya and accepts this boy, he makes the request through the yobidashi-kai (Association of yobidashi) to the JSA. Of course, this can be done only if there is a vacancy. If the 45 yobidashi places are filled, the master and the boy must wait for a vacancy to arise.

9.3 Do the yobidashi have ranks?

Yes, they do; exactly the same as the rikishi and the gyoji. But whereas the gyoji add '-kaku' (rank) to the name of the rank, the yobidashi do not. So you have, for instance, a juryo-kaku gyoji, but a juryo yobidashi.

The ranking of yobidashi has been official only since January 1994. Before that, the JSA did not concern itself with the internal organization of the yobidashi, who however ranked themselves inside their own (then) informal organization.

9.4 What are the ranks?

Starting at the bottom, and with qualifications where applicable:

Jonokuchi yobidashi

Jonidan yobidashi

Sandanme yobidashi

Makushita yobidashi

Juryo yobidashi (those with at least 15 years' experience, or men of particular excellence with at least 10 years' experience)

Makuuchi yobidashi (30-plus years' experience, or 15-plus years' excellent record)

Sanyaku yobidashi (40 years-plus, or at least 30 years' excellent record)

Fuku-tate yobidashi (as sanyaku)

Tate yobidashi (as sanyaku)

9.5 How are yobidashi promoted?

Generally on the basis of age and experience, although it is possible for a bright man to overtake those less able.

The promotions (and, possibly, demotions) are decided once a year, at a meeting of the rijikai (Board of Directors) held after the aki basho in September on the basis of a written report.

9.6 Is there a fixed number of yobidashi at each level?

Only for those of juryo class and above.

This is a table of the numbers permitted, and the actual numbers as of March 2003:

Tate yobidashi	1	1
Fuku-tate yobidashi	1	0
Sanyaku yobidashi	3	4
Makuuchi yobidashi	7	7
Juryo yobidashi	8	8
Makushita yobidashi		5
Sandanme yobidashi		4
Jonidan yobidashi		4
Jonokuchi yobidashi		5

9.7 Do yobidashi announce bouts of the same level as their rank?

In principle, yes; the tate yobidashi, like the tate-gyoji, is concerned with only the final bout of the day, and all the others of sekitori status announces two bouts each. At the lower levels, the number of bouts diminishes with the rise in rank.

9.8 What is the correct way to refer to a yobidashi?

Simply by putting 'yobidashi' before their given name. Their surnames are not used professionally, and they mostly have a personal name assigned to them by the stablemaster or a senior yobidashi in their heya or ichimon.

9.9 Do yobidashi have a retirement age?

Yes; like all other JSA members and employees, they must retire when they reach their 65th birthday. Strictly speaking the retirement is counted from the end of the preceding basho.

This means, according to yobidashi lore, that if a man joins at age 18 and is promoted in the regular way, he will have the qualifications to become chief yobidashi at age 58 (although men of talent may reach this level earlier); but if a man joins at age 17, that is, a year earlier, he will not become a tate-yobidashi unless he has some special excellence. Nowadays, however, almost all yobidashi come in at 15-16, after finishing middle school.

9.10 What do the yobidashi do?

The yobidashi have three main jobs: calling contestants' names, making and maintaining the dohyo, and drumming, though these are by no means all the tasks done by these busy men.

9.11 Making the dohyo (see UNIT 3, The Dohyo)

9.12 Maintaining the dohyo

Daily maintenance includes sweeping and dribbling a little water on the dohyo each time there is a change of judges' shift (roughly every hour); and at the directions of one of the judges or a senior yobidashi, removing with shovels any excess of sand and salt and bringing in fresh clean sand. The watering is extremely important: if too much water is used, the surface becomes slippery; or too little, the surface begins to break up. The most difficult place for keeping a dohyo in sound condition is Nagoya, where the air-conditioning is fierce. At the very end of the sumo day, a yobidashi repaints the two white shikiri-sen lines.

Yobidashi are also responsible for ensuring correct behavior around the dohyo. A judge or a senior yobidashi may send a junior to warn members of the public who are in the front seats not to eat, drink, smoke, lie down, or turn their back to the dohyo. Naturally, the people who really own these seats would not behave like that — but early in the day, other people often sit in these excellent seats and are not thrown out unless they make a nuisance of themselves. Another rule is that small children, even with their parents, are not allowed in the front two rows. This is for their own safety.

9.13 Calling contestants' names (yobi-age)

A bout is announced three times: by the yobidashi, by the gyoji, and finally by the gyoji at the microphone. Whichever side is going first that day, east or west (east — higashi — first on odd-numbered days, west — nishi — first on even-numbered days), the yobidashi on duty steps up from the opposite side, walks across to face the contestant, slowly opening a white folding fan. He holds the fan at arm's length in front of him, and looking over it, intones, 'higa—shi, Takanoha—na—'; then turning and taking a step or two to the other side, 'ni—shi—, Musashi—ma—ru—.' All yobidashi use the same little tune, but each man adds his own flourishes. Right from the very lowest ranks, the rikishi have their shikona called in this way. The only difference is for the sanyaku and yokozuna bouts, when each name is called twice. The yobidashi who is announcing holds concealed in his left hand a program, folded small and showing just the strip of names that he is to call. As he finishes his turn, he hands the folded program over to the yobidashi who will take over the announcing. In practice it is only the lower-ranked yobidashi, who have to call many names, who need refresh their memory.

9.14 Salt, chikara-mizu, chikara-gami

At the beginning of the day, young yobidashi prepare the salt that will be used much later, rubbing it by hand through a sieve so that there are no dangerous lumps. It goes into a large box in the hanamichi at each side, and when the salt is finally needed on the dohyo corners, it is put into boxes of woven bamboo.

During the bouts of the top two divisions, a very young yobidashi on each side is told to keep the boxes topped up, and he can sometimes be seen coming in with the salt in a plastic bowl.

Yobidashi are also responsible for bringing in the water used by the sekitori for a purificatory mouth rinse before their bouts. In the hot season, they add ice.

They also keep a supply of paper for the rikishi to hold in front of their mouths as they spit out the water.

9.15 Mizu-tsuke (water-bucket duty)

For juryo and makuuchi bouts, two junior yobidashi sit at the rear corners of the dohyo in charge of the cedar-wood buckets (mizu-oke) of water with the bamboo dippers, the woven bamboo boxes of salt, the hand-towels of the rikishi now on or at the dohyo, and a broom for last-minute tidying of the dohyo. The envelopes of prize money for the makuuchi bouts are in an open box in the care of the yobdashi on the rear/west corner. mizu-tsuke yobidashi must be exceedingly alert, for if the rikishi come hurtling off the dohyo in their direction they must pick up the bucket and move it out of harm's way. The salt occasionally goes flying, but the customers in the ringside seats can easily brush off a little salt; a gallon or so of cold water would be less easy to laugh off — and the bucket itself could cause injury to a rikishi who fell on it.

9.16 Seigen jikan desu: — 'Time's up!'

The two yobidashi on mizu-tsuke duty also have the job of telling the contestants when the time-limit for warm-up has expired (seigen jikan). They must keep looking at the time-keeping judge (5.11) who raises his right hand to chest level as a sign that the next time the rikishi return to the corners for salt, the yobidashi will rise, tell them 'seigen jikan desu,' and offer them their hand-towels.

9.17 Managing the towels

The towel of the man now on the dohyo is on top of the bucket handle; that of the next is on the near side of the folded-back bucket lid; the towel of the man just entering is on the outer part of the lid. The yobidashi must keep to the system. As a rikishi goes out after his bout, the yobidashi unobtrusively slips the towel into the man's hand. (Even a yokozuna carries his own towel until he gets to where his tsukebito is waiting.)

9.18 Parading kensho banners around the dohyo

At makuuchi level, sponsors can offer prize money for individual bouts. These prizes are called kensho, and they are advertised by yobidashi stepping up on the dohyo and carrying sponsors' banners around the outside of the circle while the names are read out on the house broadcasting system. They have to be careful of their timing, so as not to get in the way of the gyoji as he announces the bout or the rikishi as they return to their corners for salt. If there are too many banners to fit in, the remaining yobidashi have to wait for the rikishi to go to the corners and return to the center of the ring before parading the remaining banners.

9.19 Guarding kensho envelopes and handing to gyoji

The kensho (prize money) envelopes create an extra responsibility for the yobidashi at the rear/west corner (on the right as viewed from the front). The envelopes, each containing 30,000 yen, and tied in a bundle if several are offered for the same bout, are stacked neatly in an open box that is leant up against the rear of the dohyo, in easy reach of the yobidashi. As soon as the bout is decided, the yobidashi takes the envelope(s) and hands them up to the gyoji, who acclaims the winner and then hands the envelopes to him on top of his gunbai.

When the winner gets down and waits to give the next man up the water of power, the yobidashi takes his sagari (2.30) and threads the stiffened spikes through the twine holding the envelopes together. When the winner has presented the water, he takes the hammer-like bundle, along with his own hand-towel, and leaves for the changing room.

In case the winner has to return to sit beside the judge (kachi-nokori, 4.12), an unassigned yobidashi comes from the hanamichi to take the bundle from him and pass it on to the man's waiting tsukebito.

Note: In May 2012, the prize money (kensho kin) increased from 60,000 yen to 62,000 yen, but 30,000 yen is still enclosed in the envelope.

9.20 Changing Makuuchi rikishi's basho zabutons

One of the privileges of the top division rikishi is that they have their own personalized cushions to sit on while waiting their turn at the foot of the dohyo. Changing these zabuton is the job of the two yobidashi sitting at the rear corners in charge of the water, paper and salt. This is what happens at each side: As a rikishi mounts the dohyo for his bout, the tsukebito (2.12) of the next man to come in will bring in his zabuton to the foot of the hanamichi and hand it over to the yobidashi at the corner. The yobidashi goes to the vacated zabuton, dexterously switches it for the new one, and carries the old one to where the tsukebito is squatting, hopefully not blocking the view of the audience. He carries the zabuton up the hanamichi to where the tsukebito of the man now on the dohyo is waiting to take it from him.

9.21 Waiting on the judges sitting below the dohyo

If a monoii (7.7-7.8) is called, the judges rise and mount the dohyo for the discussion. When this happens, young yobidashi assigned to the duty rush around to each judge's seat and wait to help him seat himself in comfort when he gets down off the dohyo and neatly line up his zori sandals beside his cushion. Formerly the judges wore a cloth over their knees to keep off the sand, and this was set straight by the yobidashi.

One bout before a change of judges, a yobidashi calls 'kotai desu!' ('It's the change!') and the same young yobidashi move around to their appointed places to help the judge put on his sandals and straighten his garments.

All the young yobidashi must always be alert in case one of the judges calls them to carry out an order - for example, moving a small child from the front two rows, or telling someone not to smoke or drink in the front six rows.

Note: Since January 2005, smoking has been prohibited anywhere inside the Kokugi-kan. No smoking is allowed anywhere on the premises.

9.22 Injury on the dohyo

When a rikishi is injured on the dohyo, it is the job of the yobidashi to help him down. If he cannot walk, it may take several much smaller yobidashi to lift him off. At the foot of the dohyo, it becomes the job of the wakaimono-gashira (Unit 10) to take him out to the clinic, in a wheelchair or on a stretcher if necessary.

When such an accident happens, a yobidashi also picks up the salt basket, walks round the base of the dohyo to the spot nearest to where the man fell, and throw a generous handful of salt onto the place.

Similarly, if any blood falls onto the dohyo, from a nosebleed or a scratch, the dohyo's purity is spoilt. So a yobidashi rubs away all trace of the blood with one or more sheets of paper (chikara-gami 4.22) and then sprinkles salt on the place.

9.23 Regular announcements by banner

If a rikishi fails to arrive for his bout (usually through sending a message that he is sick or injured), a yobidashi steps up and shows to the four sides a white banner bearing the words 'fusensho' — win by forfeit.

There is also a banner announcing a mizu-iri (8.41) — a break for a rest when a bout has gone on for about four minutes and appears to have no prospect of a quick end. The banner reads 'Fresh bout after the next two bouts.' The rikishi return to the changing rooms for about five minutes of rest, then walk back in while the yobidashi holds up another banner: 'From before, fresh bout.'

9.24 Assisting the chief gyoji with kao-bure gonjou

Between the yokozuna dohyo-iri and the start of the makuuchi matches, there is usually a gap of 15-20 minutes, during which the chief gyoji reads out the pairings for the next day (kao-bure gonjo 8.52). He is assisted by a junior yobidashi who squats a little behind him on his left, to take from him each page that contains two men's names and turn it dexterously to face each side of the audience.

9.25 Waiting on JSA officials in yakuin-shitsu

During a hon-basho, young yobidashi are also on duty in the yakuin-shitsu — the office for the JSA officials (yakuin), to run errands for them.

9.26 General help in the heya

Yobidashi also have to help the heya to which they are affiliated in many ways. On a quiet day, they may serve tea to important visitors watching training. As members of an ichimon (7.3), the younger ones must work together to do the specialist work needed for making the training dohyo in all the heya in the ichimon. The apprentice rikishi are used for the rough work, but only a yobidashi can make the tawara (3.21) and fit them in smoothly.

In former times it was the yobidashi who, on jungyo tours, did the cooking for the oyakata.

Section 2 YOBIDASHI 2 Dress and equipments

9.27 What is the yobidashi's costume ?

Oddly enough, the JSA does not make any stipulations about what the yobidashi should wear, but their outfit has been fixed by custom: over a cotton yukata or a kimono, they wear tattsuke-bakama, pants that have only front and back but no sides as they hang from the cloth belt. They are baggy at the knees (for a full-length kimono is tucked into the baggy part); below the knees a cloth flap wraps tightly around the calf forming leggings. On their feet they wear dark jika-tabi, cloth shoes that are like the tabi socks worn by gyoji of juryo rank and above; but because yobidashi walk a lot on the sandy, gritty dohyo, their tabi have rubber (or these days plastic) soles. These soles are soft enough that they do not damage the dohyo surface. During tournament time yobidashi wear kimono bearing sponsors' advertising printed on the back.

Away from the dohyo they may wear happi, loose-fitting jackets of printed or dyed cotton or silk, usually bearing the name of a heya or rikishi. For the fure-daiko (9.37) played on the day before a basho opens, they have a different dress entirely: white close-fitting pants, yukata with a front corner drawn up and tucked into the waistband, and a happi jacket.

9.28 Does the yobidashi's costume vary with rank?

No, not at all.

9.29 Who provides the yobidashi's costumes?

They mostly receive them from sponsors or benefactors. The kimono in particular mostly come from commercial enterprises — Japanese-style snack and insurance companies seem to be the most common — and the names are printed in large characters on the back of the kimono, making the yobidashi walking billboards. The pants, navy blue with vertical stripes, are made of silk (a light weave, ro, for summer and a heavier one, hitokoshi, for winter), and are often presented by a rikishi when he is promoted to ozeki or yokozuna. In this case they will have the name of the rikishi embroidered on the tab that sticks up at the back.

The custom of sponsors' providing the costumes dates from the hard days immediately after the end of World War II, when the yobidashi were glad to have good clothes given to them, even if they did carry advertising. In these more affluent days many yobidashi feel that it should be below their dignity to advertise insurance and little fishy munchies — but the custom is firmly entrenched. For events such as retirement ceremonies, however, the yobidashi wear yukata or kimonos of their own, or presented by the retiree or his stable.

9.30 Is the yobidashi's white fan special? (Sensu)

Yes, it is. Although it looks like any other plain white paper folding fan with wooden ribs, it has silk in the paper and is made a little larger than normal, and the part held in the hand has a piece of lead inserted into it for balance.

9.31 Who provides the white fans?

A particular member of the Tokyo tamarikai (11.10) has been presenting, as a regular custom, 15 or these fans at each Tokyo basho. These are saved up till the third basho, when the total comes to 45 — one for each yobidashi.

9.32 Do the fans differ according to the yobidashi's rank?

No; they are all exactly the same.

9.33 Is anything written on the fans?

No. They are absolutely plain.

9.34 What are those clappers they use? (ki or hyoshigi)

Each yobidashi has his own set of ki, a pair of wooden blocks, convex-curved in cross-section, and linked by a cord at one end. They are struck together to produce a sharp clear tone that resounds through the Kokugikan. The technique has to be acquired, but the trick lies in bringing the base of the blocks together fractionally before the upper ends. Cherry wood is favored, from the reddish heart of the log, but any close-grained wood can be used.

The sharp clacking of the ki punctuates the sumo day.

Ichiban-gi (first clappers): 30 minutes before the first bout of the day is due to start, two junior yobidashi go to the east and west shitaku-beya (changing rooms) to warn rikishi to get ready; 15 minutes before, niban-gi (second clappers) is sounded.Then, as the first shift of judges walks in, one yobidashi sounds his clappers inside the hall itself, to signal the official start of the day. Ki are also beaten as the judges walk in to start the juryo bouts, and again for the makuuchi bouts.

Yoi-no-ki (warning clappers): about 10 minutes before a dohyo-iri, two young yobidashi with about 2-3 years' experience go to the shitaku-beya to warn the juryo to put on their keshô-mawashi ready for the ring-entering ceremony. The yobidashi check the time with the wakaimono-gashira (Unit 10) on duty.

The ki are used in the dohyo-iri to give the rikishi their timing. A yobidashi with about ten years' experience stands at the corner of the dohyo and strikes the clappers in slow rhythmic beats. He takes his timing from the gyoji (12.6) who is announcing the names. On one beat the next rikishi moves forward, and on the next, climbs up onto the dohyo. When it is the last man's time, the yobidashi speeds up the beat to warn the men standing in the circle that it is time to turn and face inwards. He resumes the beat as they file out, speeding up as the disappear from view. Suddenly a new sound begins to take over, as another yobidashi rises at the opposite corner and does the same thing.

When a yokozuna comes in to perform his dohyo-iri, he is led in by the chief yobidashi beating his clappers, which are also used to emphasize parts of the ceremony itself.

Ki also add dignity and emphasis to other important parts of the day: before announcement of the final juryo bout, and that of the musubi-no-ichiban; and hane-gi, before and after the yumitori-shiki (comparable with hane-daiko 9.37).

9.35 Who provides the wooden clappers?

The yobidashi themselves mostly provide their own ki. Each yobidashi has his own pair of wooden blocks, which remain his personal possession. They are made of cherry wood, and the best material is the reddish heart of the tree-trunk. It is said that they produce a better sound if the blocks are made from two different trees.

9.36 Is there any special technique of striking the blocks?

Yes; unlike the stage use (in Kabuki or Bunraku theater, for instance), the sumo clappers are not brought together from an outside position. Instead, one is held still and the other brought to meet it. A bottom-to-top movement can often be observed.

9.37 What is the purpose of beating the drum 'taiko'?

The taiko is a double-headed drum used in Japanese folk music and dancing as well as to liven up sumo occasions. The yobidashi use several different drumming rhythms depending on the occasion: fure-daiko, yagura-daiko, yose-daiko, hane-daiko and others.

Fure-daiko is played the day before a basho: at the end of the dohyo-matsuri (8.52.a), two groups of yobidashi with taiko slung from poles walk three times around the newly-consecrated dohyo, with a man beating each head of the drum. For the rest of the day, groups of yobidashi make their way around all the sumo-beya and other places (restaurants and coffee-shops for instance) that have invited them, stopping at each to sing out the first day's top-division bouts, with fure-daiko drumming before and after. To enable them to form more groups, they hire laborers to carry the pole from which the taiko is slung .

The taiko is played from the top of the yagura, a tall drum-tower in front of the Kokugikan. The Tokyo yagura, some 16 meters tall, is now a permanent structure of metal, but until May 1995 it was put up before each basho using long wooden poles and straw string. Outside of Tokyo this old construction method is still used. Two young yobidashi play the taiko, one on the head and one on the wooden body. If the weather is bad, they do not go up the drum-tower but instead kneel on cushions under the second-floor projecting roof.

Yose-daiko is played from 8.00 to 8.30 on mornings when sumo is held. These days it simply adds a bit of color and cheers the people waiting to buy tickets; in former times, when open-air tournaments were postponed if it rained, the drumming was needed to announce that sumo would really be taking place that day.

Hane-daiko is played at the end of the day, to give the departing spectators the feeling that the day is not quite over; though it is said to be intended as an invitation to come back the next day.

9.38 How do young yobidashi learn their many jobs?

Their seniors in the heya or ichimon usually give the new yobidashi informal lessons in calling and beating the blocks, which are skills needed straight away. If you go into the stadium as soon as the doors open, long before the bouts are scheduled to commence, you may see the new intake of yobidashi receiving their first lessons in calling (yobi-age) actually on the dohyo, with half-a-dozen yobidashi 'teachers' not much older shouting advice from below the dohyo.

For drumming lessons, senior yobidashi pass on their skills in the yobidashis' dressing room in the Kokugikan. These lessons go on until the young yobidashi reaches the sandanme level. In the old days no such instruction was given, and the youngsters were expected to learn by imitation — 'stealing knowledge,' it was called.

Periodically lessons in calling and drumming are given to all the younger yobidashi on the dohyo.

It is also said that, since yobidashi do so many things as a group, the young yobidashi pick up much of what they know without consciously studying it.

9.39 How do yobidashi help out in their heya?

General help. They run errands for the master, they greet and see off guests, answer the phone, bring tea, and such jobs. If there is a party in the heya, the yobidashi are likely to be outside the door, in charge of storing the guests' shoes — whereas the socially superior gyoji will be inside, manning the reception desk, taking in money and keeping the accounts.

9.40 Who do yobidashi eat with?

It varies from heya to heya; but in general they make little or no distinction of rank.

9.41 How much does a yobidashi earn?

The yobidashi's income, like the gyoji's, is in two parts: the basic and the allowance.

This is a table of the basic salary (hon-po):

    1. Jonokuchi yobidashi   ¥14,000-20,000

2. Jonidan yobidashi	¥20,000-29,000
3. Sandanme yobidashi	¥29,000-42,000
4. Makushita yobidashi	¥42,000-100,000
5. Juryo yobidashi	¥100,000-200,000
6. Makuuchi yobidashi	¥200,000-360,000
7. Sanyaku yobidashi	¥360,000-400,000
8. Fuku-tate yobidashi	¥360,000-400,000
9. Tate yobidashi	¥360,000-400,000

but these very low salaries, especially in the junior ranks, are supplemented by much larger 'allowances' (teate).

For the lowest rank, jonokuchi yobidashi, the sum looks like this:

basic salary	¥14,000
allowance	¥126,000
total	¥140,000

9.42 Is there any special treatment for long service?

After 30 years' service, a yobidashi is classified as 'qualified' (yu-shikakusha) and gets the same treatment, in transportation, accommodation, etc., as rikishi of juryo level. His salary is also at much the same level as that of a juryo rikishi. In other words, what used to be a subsistence job has now become a proper career.

UNIT 10 OTHER SUPPORTING PLAYERS

Section 1 WAKAIMONO-GASHIRA

10.1 What does 'wakaimono-gashira' mean?

'Kashira' means 'head,' and 'wakai-mono' is a young person. So literally the eight wakaimono-gashira are in charge of the young rikishi. (In ordinary Japanese the pronunciation is 'wakamono' but the sumo people prefer the old-fashioned way.) They are usually addressed as 'kashira.'

10.2 What do the wakaimono-gashira do?

In general they supervise and guide rikishi below sekitori rank; in practice nearly all the instruction and advice, both in sumo matters and general life, are directed toward the very youngest apprentices. Wakaimono-gashira, or kashira for short, have certain specific, and important, jobs. Let's take a look at them in descending order of visibility.

1) On senshuraku, when play-offs (kettei-sen) are needed to decide the championships in the juryo and lower ranks, they stand at the foot of the dohyo and organize the draw for play-offs (10.2) at the end of the regular juryo bouts. After the musubi-no-ichiban (8.11), if a multiple play-off is needed for the supreme championship, some of the kashira come in again and organize the draw for the order of play.

2) Also on senshuraku, they are in charge of getting the trophies and certificates in the right order for the presentation and, very noticeably, receiving them from

the championship winner and carrying them up the hanamichi to where the man's tsukebito are waiting to take them.

3) From Day 3 of a basho, they run the mae-zumo, the preliminary bouts that are the only mode of entry into professional sumo. All eight kashira are present. They have a record of who meets whom, and enter the results; they make sure that the boys are waiting on the correct side and also get off on the correct side. Before the boys even enter the hall, they also make sure their mawashi are tied properly; and they instruct them in how and when to bow and make other gestures of courtesy.

4) When the boys are through mae-zumo, they are dressed in borrowed kesho-mawashi (put on by the kashira) and paraded in and presented to the public in the shinjo shusse hiro (1.18) .When the simple ceremony is over, the kashira more or less manhandle them down off the dohyo at the front/west corner and take them round the various offices in the Kokugikan to make a bow and announce their name to the oyakata and others.

5) Each day of a hon-basho, a kashira is responsible for the envelopes of prize money (kenshokin) which are inscribed with the name of the corporate donor and sorted into bundles according to which bout they are placed on; the kashira finally puts the bundles in order in a box which will be handed over to the yobidashi on mizu-tsuke duty (9.15) at the west side.

6) During hon-basho, there are kashira on duty the whole day from 7.30. There are always two of them sitting in the hall on the east and west sides, not particularly watching the sumo but available in case of injury. They are relieved by another pair at the same time as the judges (shinpan) change shifts. If an injury occurs on the dohyo, the yobidashi help the man down, after which it is the job of the wakaimono-gashira to help him out. Sometimes he is carried piggy-back, sometimes wheeled out in a chair or on a stretcher. The kashira then take him first

to the Sumo Clinic in the basement, from where he may be routed to a hospital. In this case, a kashira goes with him.

7) It is also the duty of the kashira to collect and report to the Judges' Department and the Kyokai office each day the names of any rikishi in their heya or ichimon who are unable to appear for a bout through sickness or injury. Out of basho time, they are the ones who take the sick and injured from their own heya to hospital and go through the formalities. In their free time, the kashira are also expected to visit rikishi in hospital.

8) The responsibility from which they get their title is supervising the underage rikishi, and this starts at the very beginning of their careers, when a kashira representing his stablemaster exchanges contracts with a boy's parents and quite possibly takes him back there and then to the heya. (As there are some 50 heya and only eight wakaimono-gashira, obviously this job is also done by others. See 10.3 below)

Note: The number of sumo-beya sometimes varies for a number of reasons. As of February 2022, there are 43.

9) Their first job with new entrants is to teach them reigi — basic sumo manners. 'Don't speak unless you are spoken to; when a senior speaks to you, answer promptly; carry out instructions willingly; keep your person neat and clean; keep your finger and toe nails trimmed.' This last is not merely for appearance but to prevent a sharp nail from scratching an opponent. The kashira may also give simple lessons in basic sumo, although this varies from heya to heya. They also sell rolls of tape, used for binding fingers together to safeguard them in training.

10) Shin-deshi kensa: In the week before a hon-basho starts, the new apprentices (shin-deshi) are put through a series of examinations and tests (1.4, 1.8) which are

carried out by doctors, nurses and various oyakata; the kashira are responsible for the general running of the event, seeing that the boys are correctly lined up and their names properly recorded.

11) On jungyo (tours, 3.38) and at charity and retirement performances (hana-zumo) the kashira have rather wider duties which may include supervising the line-up of the bouts.

12) In the heya, the kashira, like the gyoji, may carry out secretarial duties for the master, such as mailing the banzuke to the supporters an adjusting the itineraries of the sekitori. The difference is that the gyoji does the calligraphy while the kashira is more likely to do the ordinary clerical jobs.

13) Their least-known job is probably the rare one of consulting with a yokozuna and his stablemaster about recommending to the JSA officials a new man to perform the yumitori-shiki (bow-twirling ceremony, 2.38).

10.3 Do wakaimono-gashira work equally for all heya?

No; there are only eight of them, and there are usually around 50 sumo-beya. So the majority of heya do not have a kashira. They may make up the lack in various ways. One of the commonest solutions these days is to hire a 'manager' (the English word is used with Japanese pronunciation), usually a former makushita rikishi like a kashira, and doing much the same work as far as the heya is concerned. Unlike the kashira, however, he is paid by the stablemaster and is not a JSA employee.

10.4 How does a man become a wakaimono-gashira?

See 10:7 below. Typically, he used to be a man who had spent a long time in makushita, maybe having briefly been promoted to juryo; but in recent years there have been cases even of former makuuchi men who decided to become kashira rather than drop out of sumo when their active life ended and they had not obtained a myoseki (13.2). Often the successful applicant has spent time as a trainer in the sumo school, where he showed kindliness and firmness, and a man has proven his worth and is widely respected and liked.

Section 2 SEWANIN

10.5 What does 'sewanin' mean?

'Sewa' means literally 'service' and 'nin' is a word for 'person'; so the sewanin is literally a 'useful person' — a man who makes himself useful.

10.6 What does a sewanin do?

The eight sewanin are primarily responsible for the equipment needed for staging a public performance of sumo. They also act as back-ups for the wakaimono-gashira, and as general support staff. In particular, they can be seen doing the following jobs:

1) Transportation and care of equipment; on jungyo, they supervise the loading and unloading of the trucks or other transportation, put up tents as needed, and in general make themselves useful.

2) During hon-basho, they supervise the changing rooms (shitaku-beya) and may guard the entrances to them.

3) Early in the day, they may take a turn tearing tickets at the entrance for the

general public. Strictly speaking, this is the task of various oyakata, but a sewanin may be asked to relieve one.

4) A sewanin may be responsible for the switches that control the red lights on the electric scoreboard.

5) Supervision of the car park.

6) Assist in the officials' office (yakuin-shitsu).

10.7 How does a man become a wakaimono-gashira or a sewanin?

When a vacancy arises, a written recommendation is made bearing the names and seals of all the oyakata in his ichimon. The appointment is eventually made by the Board of Directors.

10.8 Do wakaimono-gashira and sewanin wear a special uniform?

When on duty they normally wear the navy blue blouson issued to all Kyokai members and employees, but otherwise they wear their own clothes. For the play-offs and the trophy presentations on the final day of a hon-basho, the kashira who appear in view of the cameras take care to wear good suits.

10.9 How about salaries?

These two classes of men get paid in the same way as other JSA employees: a very small sum in basic salary and an allowance that brings it up to a living wage.

Section 3 TOKOYAMA AND MAGE

10. 10 What is the tokoyama's work?

The tokoyama's work is to create and take care of the mage, the clubbed hair styles that are the symbol of the professional rikishi. He does nothing else — but because the rikishi have to have their long hair dressed at least once every day, it is hard for him to take a holiday.

10.11 What is the mage?

The mage is a topknot, or a club of hair worn on top of the head. The custom of oiling the hair of both men and women and clubbing it together in various styles dates back to prehistoric times in Japan, as we can see from old statuettes. At the beginning of the Meiji period, all Japanese men had much the same kind of hair style. Then, as part of Japan's efforts to modernize as rapidly as possible, there was enacted in 1871 the danpatsu-rei, the Hair-cut Law, which decreed that all Japanese men were to have western-style hair-cuts — except the sumo wrestlers, who were considered to embody a part of Japanese tradition that could not be modernized without destroying its character.

10.12 What are the two styles?

The chon-mage and the o-icho-mage. The chon-mage, a simple club, is worn by all rikishi for normal life; for formal occasions such as hon-basho appearances, weddings and ceremonial retirement hair-cuttings, the sekitori (juryo and above) have the more elaborate o-icho, so called from its resemblance to a semicircular ginkgo leaf.

10.13 How is the chon-mage formed?

The hair is combed out and oiled, and then drawn back into a clump at the crown of the head and tied near the scalp with a length of paper string called motoyui. The club of hair is bent over and a second loop of the string is passed around the doubled-over part. The tokoyama keeps the string taut in his teeth, as both his hands are occupied. When everything is in place, he leans forward and bites off the surplus string. The mage is brought forward and curved slightly to the left. Nothing keeps it in place but the oil.

10.14 When is an apprentice allowed to have a chon-mage?

As soon as his hair is long enough. Most new entrants come from country schools where a very short cut is the rule. As the hair begins to grow, they first look like bottle-brushes, then their heads are a shaggy mass (zanbara-gami), and finally the great day arrives when the ends of the hair can be brought together to meet under the chin. This rough-and-ready measure means that it is long enough for the tokoyama to form a small mage. It is a time for celebration. All the oyakata in the heya give the young man a painful flick of the thumb-nail on the forehead — and then sweeten the pain with a generous gift of money.

10.15 How is the o-icho-mage formed?

The hair is drawn into a club as for the chon-mage, but the formal style requires another two or three inches (8-10 cm) of hair growth because, instead of the hair being drawn tight over the skull, it is fanned out into a sort of bag shape and then formed into a sharp edge with a thin steel rod — the mage-bo. After years of use, the tip of the mage-bo gets worn down, so a veteran tokoyama's mage-bo may be an inch shorter than a new instrument. The mage is bent over and tied with paper string as before, but the end of the hair is molded into an upstanding semi-circle that is thought to resemble the ginkgo leaf.

In the Edo period there were additional shapes of mage: the kuri-mage (chestnut) and the yagura-mage (tower), for instance.

10.16 Does the mage have any practical use?

It seems that every sumo book has to contain the information that the mage acts as a cushion in case of a fall; but common sense and simple observation indicate that a man hardly ever falls on the top of his head.

10.17 What is the nakazori?

If a rikishi's hair is very thick, it is difficult to make the mage sit well, so the tokoyama shaves a small circular patch on the top of the scalp just in front of the place where the mage is bent forward. This little shaven patch is the nakazori. If an aging sekitori tells a tokoyama not to shave his scalp, he is likely to be thinking of retirement; for a shaven patch will show up under a modern haircut.

10.18 What are the tools of the trade?

The tokoyama uses seven items:

> ara-gushi: a long narrow comb for the first combing
> suki-gushi: a short squat comb for removing bits of loose hair
> soroe-gushi: a large comb for forming the mage
> motoyui: waxed string made from washi, Japanese-style paper
> mage-bo: a thin steel rod with a wooden handle, for forming the flared base
>   of the o-icho style

mae-gaki: a very thin comb for smoothing the front of the hair

suki-abura: hardened oil in a round flat box; it looks like colorless shoe polish

bintsuke-abura: the same kind of grease but in stick form, for applying to the sides and temples

One particular manufacturer in the Nagoya area makes all the combs used in professional sumo, and all the tokoyama go there ahead of the sumo contingent to buy a year's supply at a time. Each comb is cut from a single piece of boxwood (tsuge-gushi).

10.19 What are the parts of the hair called?

The bin is the side hair; the tabo is the back hair flared out from the scalp; and the mage is the clubbed part.

10.20 How does a boy become a tokoyama?

Although tokoyama are employees of the JSA, recruitment is done through the master of a heya, who applies to the rijikai, Board of Directors. The basic qualifications are exactly the same as for gyoji and yobidashi, and there is a fixed number: in this case, 50. If there are already 50 tokoyama, an application has to be put on hold. In cases where the number of sumo-beya increases further, the Kyokai may permit the recruitment of two or three extra apprentice tokoyama.

10.21 Does every heya have a tokoyama?

No; although 50 tokoyama for around 50 heya looks like a tidy fit, in fact some large heya have three or four tokoyama while some small heya have none. When a sumo-beya has no tokoyama, it has to borrow one from another heya in the ichimon, either by having him come around or by sending its rikishi to the other heya after training.

10.22 Does a small heya pay to hire a tokoyama from elsewhere?

There is nothing fixed by the rules, but in practice such a visiting tokoyama can expect some private payment for the extra work. And behind the scenes at public appearances, tokoyama will help out anyone in their ichimon.

10.23 Is a tokoyama the same as a barber or hairdresser?

No, there is no resemblance. The tokoyama's job is descended from the tokoya of the Edo period, who dressed everybody's hair. After the danpatsu-rei of 1871 (10.11), the tokoya went out of business and only the worlds of kabuki and sumo still needed this kind of professional. During WWII the profession almost died out in sumo, too, and after the war, it is said, some of the kabuki hairdressers trained new ones for sumo. The kabuki hairdressers and wig-dressers had always been called tokoyama to distinguish them from the everyday tokoya, and because of this kabuki training, the sumo tokoyama took the kabuki name.

10.24 How does a tokoyama learn his trade?

From a senior in the heya or the ichimon. There is no formal training or school for tokoyama.

10.25 Do tokoyama have ranks or classes?

Yes, depending on length of experience. They are:

Grade 1: 30 years' experience and over
Grade 2: 20 years and over

Grade 3: 10 years and over

Grade 4: 5 years and over

Grade 5: 3 years and over

Minarai (Apprentice) less than 3 years

> Note 1: Only Grades 1 and 2 are qualified to do the o-icho style; but the tokoyama themselves say that they can do it after 7-10 years' experience, and sometimes a   new heya produces a sekitori long before its tokoyama reaches Grade 2.

> Note 2: Sometimes a tokoyama of Grade 1 may be raised to a special class, but this is above the regular grades, and is a mark of excellence as well as long service.

10.26 Do tokoyama have special names?

Every tokoyama's name begins with 'toko-.' The second part is commonly taken from his own given or family name, but there is no rule at all; the master may add part of the heya's name, his own fighting name, or anything else he chooses.

10.27 When does a tokoyama dress the hair?

Usually when the rikishi come from their bath after a training session. During hon-basho, the sekitori have the o-icho style done in the heya and travel to the sumo venue like that; the tokoyama then goes to the changing room and returns the hair to the ordinary chon-mage after the bout.

10.28 How long does it take to dress one man's hair?

The chon-mage takes no more than 5 minutes, while a skilled man can do an o-icho in 15-20 minutes. The hairdressing demonstration that is often presented at a retirement ceremony or charity performance takes no more than 10 minutes, but in this case the hair has already been combed out.

10.29 What is the hair-oil made of?

It is a very dense, greasy solid made from a mixture of sumac wax (wax-tree, Rhus silvestris) and rapeseed (kolza) oil, with a strong perfume added. When a tokoyama starts his work after a morning's training session, you can smell a sumo-beya from around the corner, so powerful is the scent.

10.30 Do foreign-born rikishi have any problems with their hair?

If they have naturally curly hair, the combing out can be very painful — but this is not confined to foreigners. There are some Japanese who also have curly hair, and they suffer just as much. Some of the Hawaiians and, unexpectedly, Mongolians, have to have a 'straight perm' to make the tokoyama's work easier and less painful.

10.31 When does the tokoyama have lunch?

There is nothing fixed, but since he cannot eat until the last rikishi's hair has been dressed, he tends to be one of the last to sit down.

10.32 What other work does the tokoyama do?

The only fixed work is dressing the hair. The rest depends on the heya and its master. Some tokoyama may also shave or massage the oyakata or the rikishi; a young tokoyama may be assigned as a tsukebito.

10.33 What sort of salary does the tokoyama earn?

It works out at very much the same as the yobidashi.

10.34 The tokoyama is always listed last among the heya personnel. Is it such a lowly job?

The tokoyama are listed after the yobidashi because their work is behind the scenes, whereas the yobidashi get up onto the dohyo. But their job is a necessary one, and it also has its privileges. Senior tokoyama get to accompany the sekitori on trips abroad. Apart from official tours, when someone like a yokozuna is visiting another country privately or to promote something, he takes a tokoyama with him as a private valet.

The tokoyama can also expect tips from senior sekitori. His calm, steady movements are usually soothing to the rikishi and put him in a calm frame of mind for his bout. When there is a play-off for the championship on senshuraku, the contestants return for 10 minutes or so to the changing rooms, where their hair is freshened up. This calms them as well as making them look like champions.

UNIT 11 HON-BASHO EVENTS (Official tournament)

11.1 What is the schedule of each day in a hon-basho?

The main characteristic is that the day starts with the bouts of the lowest ranks and the level gradually rises. There are no real intervals, but roughly every hour the judges' shift changes, and during the few minutes' wait the yobidashi sweep the dohyo and sprinkle water on it.

11.2 What time does the Kokugikan open?

These days, at 8:00, at the same time as two young yobidashi mount the yagura and beat the yose-daiko, the half-hour's drumming that welcomes the customers.

11.3 What time do the bouts start?

Starting time depends on the number of rikishi in the lowest divisions. It may be as early as 8:20 or as late as 9:00; when there are fewer bouts to be fitted in, starting time may be 8:40 or even a little later. In principle the starting time is more or less the same for each of the first 12 days; after that it is later, when the men in all four divisions below juryo have only one bout to fit into the remaining three days.

Before the official bouts on Day 3 and thereafter there is maezumo.

11.4 Is each division scheduled to start at a certain time?

No. After the opening bouts of the day, there is no fixed schedule until the juryo dohyo-iri, which is 2:40 or 2:45, except on the final day when everything is half an hour early to allow for the presentations at the end (and sometimes a play-off). That is followed by the top five makushita bouts, then all the juryo bouts. The only other event with a scheduled time is the makunchi dohyo-iri, followed by the yokozuna dohyo-iri. This is scheduled to begin at 3:50 or 3:55.

Note: The times of the juryo and makuuchi dohyo-iri are half an hour earlier on the final day, to allow time for the trophy presentations.

Finally, at the end of the day, the yumitori-shiki (bow-twirling ceremony) (12.32) is scheduled for just before 6:00. This timing is due to the exigencies of the TV programming, and has no bearing on the sumo!

11.5 Is the timing strict?

No; it is an estimate based on averages. Therefore, if it happens that a monoii (objection) is called several times, or if by chance there are many long bouts, the schedule may be quite late; on the other hand, things may go very quickly with a succession of quick decisions, and things are ahead of schedule. When things are running late, there is little that can be done except that a new shift of judges comes in very promptly. When the bouts are running early, many things can be done: a judge may order an extra sweeping of the dohyo; the incoming shift of judges may deliberately take their time; and if the makushita bouts are very early, the men in the last ten bouts before the juryo dohyo-iri will be told by a yobidashi, on the orders of a judge, to throw salt once or twice. But on average, the timing works very well.

11.6 What is the naka-iri?

This is the name given to the start of the top division events, opened by the makuuchi dohyo-iri. Between the parades and the start of the top division bouts proper, there is the only small interval of the whole day when nothing is officially scheduled. When there is time, except on the final day, the kaobure-gonjo (announcement of the next day's top division bouts) takes place.

11.7 Is every day's schedule exactly the same?

There are extra events on each of the three Sundays.

11.8 What happens on the first Sunday?

Shonichi (Day 1)

Kyokai goaisatsu: when there are three bouts still to come in the juryo division, a microphone is set up at the center front of the dohyo, and the Rijicho steps up, with all the yokozuna and sanyaku ranks lined up behind him. He reads a short — and predictable— speech, thanking people for their support, and occasionally apologizing for some shortcoming in the sumo, the absence of an important rikishi through injury, or else mentioning some good point, such as a recent ozeki or yokozuna promotion.

Return of the Emperor's Cup and the Championship Banner: Immediately after the yokozuna dohyo-iri on the first day, the winner of the previous tournament carries the Cup and the banner and hands them over to one of the chief judges (who take turns to receive them).

Unveiling of the Championship Photographs: The winners of the past two basho mount the dohyo in turn, receive a citation and then turn to face their giant photograph (yusho-gaku), which is then electronically uncovered.

11.9 What happens on the second Sunday?

Nakabi (Day 7)

Shinjo shusse hiro: The new apprentices who have passed the maezumo preliminary bouts are presented to the public. This takes place during the change of judges' shifts in the middle of the sandanme bouts. One set of judges goes out and, before the next group comes in, all the new entrants file onto the dohyo, dressed in borrowed kesho-mawashi. They squat in rows across the whole of the square and each one rises and bows as his name is called. Then a junior gyoji announces that these have passed the maezumo and from next basho will appear on the banzuke; 'please give them your favor.' On the gyoji's command, they rise, bow to the front, turn and bow to the east, then rear, west, and finally to the front again. They then dismount from the front-and-west corner of the dohyo and are led off by the wakaimono-gashira to all the offices to announce their heya and name and make their bow to all the Kyokai officials. Incidentally, the gyoji uses for this ceremony, not his own gunbai, but a white folding fan borrowed from one of the yobidashi.

Note: The presentation of the new recruits happens on nakabi in five of the six annual hon-basho. As there are far more new apprentices trying out for maezumo in Osaka, however, there are three presentations there: the first is always on Day 5, the second may be Day 8 or 9, and the third, Day 12 or 13.

11.10 What happens on the third Sunday?

Senshuraku (Day 15)

Befitting the final day, there are all sorts of 'extras.'

Kyokai goaisatsu: This happens exactly as on Day 1. The only difference is that the Rijicho's speech will mention any particularly good or bad features of the basho that is almost over.

Lower division playoffs, presentations

Directly after the final juryo bout and before the makuuchi dohyo-iri, there are (if needed) the play-offs for the championships of the lower divisions. These yusho ketteisen can be quite lengthy, as it is not uncommon for three or four, or even five or six men to have perfect 7-0 scores.

Yusho Ketteisen system

This is the same as for the main championship, but more men lead to more variations. Note: the order of bouts,and which side a man starts from, are decided by drawing slips of paper with 'East 1' 'West 1' etc. written on the part that is concealed.

- 2 finalists: simple play-off.
- 3 finalists: tomoe-sen; that is, A and B fight; if A wins, he immediately takes on C, and if he beats him also, he is the outright winner; but if C wins, then C fights B. This goes on until one man wins two successive victories.
- 4 finalists: two semifinals and a final.
- 5 finalists: one man draws a bye; two semifinals are held and then there is a tomoe-sen of the final three.
- 6 finalists: three semifinals and a tomoe-sen of the winners.
- 7 finalists: one bye, three quarterfinals, then two semifinals and a final.
- 8 finalists: four quarterfinals, two semifinals and one final.

The same principles would apply to higher numbers if necessary.

○ Presentations

A certificate is presented to the winner of each division by one of the three chief judges (who rotate this duty). After this, the same winners in the same order receive a money prize provided by the tamarikai or tozaikai, the elite group of supporters who sit in the best of the ringside seats. The presentation is customarily made by one of the gyoji in costume, though it may be done by a male representative of the association.

○ Soroi-bumi

The makuuchi bouts follow, right up to the musubi no ichiban, the final bout of the day. One small and impressive ceremony takes place three bouts before the end, when the contestants in those three final bouts mount the dohyo together, first the three on the east side, then the three on the west. The eastern three form a triangle with one man at the front and two behind; the western group have two at the front and one at the rear. Together they perform the shiko leg-raising and foot-stamping ritual.

If there is a tie at the end of the bouts on the final day, then there will be a play-off, but it is not part of the basho proper. The yumitori-shiki (bow ceremony) takes place as usual, and there is a short break while the finalists have their hair recombed and take a short rest.

○ Yusho ketteisen

If needed, this is conducted in exactly the same way as described just above. It is then followed by the presentation of trophies and awards to the yusho winner Before this, it has become customary for him to be interviewed by an NHK announcer at the foot of the dohyo.

11.11 What are all those trophies that the champion gets right at the end?

1) The Emperor's Cup: Tenno Shihai (天皇賜杯)

The origin of the Emperor's Cup, the main trophy, dates back to April 29, 1925, when a sumo performance was given at Akasaka Togu Palace in honor of the Crown Prince's birthday. The Crown Prince was a young man called Prince Hirohito, and he was Regent at that time because his father, the Taisho Emperor, was still alive but unable to perform his ceremonial duties. The Regent, who would soon become the Showa Emperor and a few years later the father of the present Emperor, presented a gift of money to the Sumo Association to thank them for the performance, which was called 台覧相撲、 tairan-zumo. The Kyokai discussed what to do with this literally princely sum, and got permission to have a large silver cup made for presentation to the individual winners of the tournaments. The first winner, in January 1926, was Tsunenohana and the cup was at first called 摂政賜杯 sessho-hai, the Regent's Cup. It has been called the Emperor's Cup since January 1928.

The names of the yusho winners are engraved on small silver labels attached to the base. The oldest are removed to a large wooden plaque to make room for new ones.

It weighs 29 kg. (64 lbs.) and can hold 36 litres of liquid — except that the lid is soldered on!

2) Yusho Banner (Yusho-ki 優勝旗)

The large purple banner, with the Kyokai's cherry blossom crest, was introduced in June 1909, at the time of the opening of the first Kokugikan. At that time the basho was still a contest between the teams of east and west, and the banner was presented to the individual with the best score on the side with the most aggregate wins. From February 1932, however, when the basho became an individual contest (not East versus West), the banner was presented to the winner along with the Emperor's Cup.

The names of the winners are hand-written on long white streamers that are attached to the top of the flagpole, with great care being taken to display the most recent winner's name on top. About two years' worth of these streamers are attached at any one time.

The Emperor's Cup and the banner are presented by one of the three chief judges at the beginning of the presentation ceremony on the final day of the basho. The two symbols are returned to the Kyokai's keeping in a sort of reverse ceremony held after the makuuchi and yokozuna dohyo-iri on the first day of the next basho. Small replicas are given to the yusho winner to keep. In the case of a famous man with a very successful career, these treasured mementos are likely to end up in a personal museum.

The present banner is the fourth. It dates from 1991 and cost about ¥9,000,000.

3) The Prime Minister's Prize
This is actually another trophy — a large silver cup that is bigger and much heavier than the Emperor's Cup. It is also more unwieldy, since the Emperor's Cup has a slender stem that affords a firm grip and a good balance.

The comparison is like this:

	Emperor's Cup	Prime Minister's Cup
Height	107 cm	85 cm
diameter	33 cm.	64 cm.
weight	29 kg.	40.8 kg.

It is traditionally presented, not by the Prime Minister in person, but by the Chief

Cabinet Secretary. A great fuss arose in 1989 when this post was held by Mayumi Moriyama, a woman, who defied the very strong sumo tradition of 'No women allowed on the dohyo' and demanded to be allowed to make the presentation — but tradition prevailed. In September 1998, Mr. Keizo Obuchi, the Prime Minister, presented it in person to Takanohana for his 20th yusho, and the present Prime Minister, Mr. Jun'ichiro Koizumi, also likes to present it in person.

4) Other prominent trophies are regularly presented, and are here given in approximate order of presentation (which varies a little). Note that the trophies remain in the Kokugikan, but most of them also carry a personal prize which the yusho winner keeps. The prefectural ones usually featured a large quantity of the local specialty, be it dried fungus or small shellfish. Many also include a sum of money. The following is the basic list.

- Czech Republic: cut glass bowl inscribed EXPO '70 EXPO, plus a year's supply of beer
- United Arab Emirates: giant coffee pot some 40 cm. tall, made of handbeaten silver with gold inlay, plus a year's supply of gasoline
- Hungary: huge red cloisonne jar, plus an individual tea-set
- China-Japan Friendship Cup: lidded cup in blue cloisonne with a design of Mount Fuji, pine and cherry blossom on a blue background
- Mongolian Prime Minister's Trophy: small but massive silver bowl on a plinth of green stone
- Mexico: large replica in silver of the Aztec calendar mounted on a wooden plaque, plus a year's supply of beer
- Tokyo Governor's Prize: statuette of a roaring lion in dull silvery metal, by the sculptor Saibo Kitamura
- Mainichi Newspapers: the real award is the giant photograph hung below the roof of the Kokugikan, but a smaller framed copy is presented now. The big one is six-mat size, i.e. the size of a regular room in a Japanese house.

- NHK Gold Cup: oval with three lengthwise flutings, based on a small cup in the Shosoin Treasure House in Nara
- Tokyo Shimbun and Chunichi Sports (two Tokyo-based newspapers): plaque (see also Sansho, 11.13)
- Zennosho (National Federation of Agricultural Cooperative Associations Prize): bronze statue of a rikishi in kesho-mawashi carrying a large gilt rice-bale; plus an actual straw bale that actually contains very little rice, so that the representative can handle it; the yusho winner actually receives 30 bales of rice, a valuable addition to his heya; plus some other delicacy such as eggs boiled in a hot spring
- Oita prefecture Shiitake Growers Cooperative: dried shiitake (a kind of oriental mushroom) in a large glass container, plus money
- Fukui prefecture: red lacquer bowl on two rice bales; plus money and a ton of umeboshi, sour pickled fruit
- Hokkaido government: bronze trophy of a giant bird, the Blakiston's fish owl; plus a truckload of produce
- Miyazaki prefecture: trophy in the form of a bull, on a stand supported by full-frontal male nudes (it weighs around 37 kilograms); carcass of prime beef
- Ehime prefecture: silver globe trophy, plus 1,500 bottles of citrus-flavored vinegar
- Shizuoka prefecture: lamp-shaped trophy: Mount Fuji above, gold paling to silver; plus the winner's weight in tea, and a gift of seasonal fruit
- Matsue City Mayor's Cup: large lidded cup plus a ton of small shellfish used in soup
- Japan Airlines (JAL): jet plane on a silver world with gold continents
- Millionaire's Cup (Ozeki sake): the giant silver sake cup later filled with sake and used in the photographs of the victor's celebrations; four barrels of sake go with it
- Isuzu Bighorn: the actual four-wheel drive vehicle stands outside the

Kokugikan for the whole basho; for the presentation, a giant plastic key is used (Coca-cola bottle, plaque representing a watch; and local ones in each venue)

Note: Although the basic information in this section was found by personal research, many details were taken from the book 'Naruhodo Ozumo' by Mr. Seigoro Kitade, a former NHK announcer. The information about the prizes is actually found in the program of bouts.

11.12 Is that the end of the last day?

No; there is still the presentation of certificates and trophies to the sansho winners.

11.13 What are the Sansho?

The three special prizes, awarded on the final day of a hon-basho. They consist of a large trophy (and a small replica which the winner keeps), and a sum of money. Currently it is ¥2 million for each prize.

11.14. What are the three prizes?

They are:

1) Kantosho (fighting spirit prize): usually given to a maegashira who has a double-digit score. It is often an encouragement to a newly-promoted man who has done unexpectedly well, and the rank of his 'victims' does not matter.

2) Shukunsho (outstanding performance prize): this award will go to a man below ozeki rank who beats yokozuna and ozeki.

3) Ginosho (technique prize): given for excellent (and varied) technique, this

tends to be the most difficult to win, and it happens sometimes that it is not awarded at all. Men in the sanyaku ranks of title-holders are most likely to win it.

11.15. Is it possible to beat a yokozuna and yet not win a Special Prize?

Yes, if a man gets make-koshi (more losses than wins), he is ineligible to win an award. But it has happened that a man won only seven real victories and his eighth was a fusensho (victory by default, when his opponent withdrew through injury); he still qualified for the award.

11.16 Can a man win more than one prize at the same time?

Yes. In November 2000, Kotomitsuki achieved the unusual feat of winning all three, as did Takahanada (later yokozuna Takanohana) in January 1992; and it often happens that a man having a good tournament is awarded two.

11.17 Can a prize be awarded to more than one man?

Yes, it is quite common for the same prize to go to two men. Each man gets the full amount of prize money.

11.18 Is there any final ceremony at the end of the Tournament?

When all the prize-giving is over, one small ceremony remains. The boys who passed maezumo line up in a circle on the dohyo, along with one of the judges. Sake is passed around to each in a shallow cup, and then, after a rhythmic hand-clapping (which is what 'teuchi' means) they all gang up to toss the judge into the air by way of celebration. It is also their only opportunity to do such a thing to an oyakata.

Note: This is called 'kamiokuri no gishiki' (which means 'seeing the gods off'). Since July 2004, a judge is no longer tossed. In his place, the newly-minted rikishi toss a juryo gyoji holding one gohei immediately after the teuchi-shiki.

UNIT 12   CEREMONIES AND PRIZES

Section 1 DOHYO-IRI — Juryo and makuuchi

The ring-entering ceremony of the juryo and the makuuchi level is exactly the same, so we will deal with both together.

12.1 What is a dohyo-iri?

It is the ceremonial entry of all the men in the division, divided into the east and west sides. A colorful spectacle, it introduces the men who will have their bouts next. They wear a special mawashi, the kesho-mawashi, which looks like a large apron (Unit 2 Section 4).

12.2 Which side goes first, east or west?

They take turns. The east side enters first on the first day of the basho and all other odd-numbered days. The west takes precedence on the even-numbered days.

12.3 Which men go on which side?

In principle they are east or west according to which side of the banzuke their names are written on. A common exception is when two men from the same side of the banzuke are to meet on the dohyo; in this case the lower-ranked man changes sides for that day.

12.4 Is there a fixed order for entering?

Yes; the men line up according to their position on the banzuke, starting with the lowest. This can be a nerve-racking experience for newly-promoted men, who have no-one to follow but must lead the way and stop in the correct place.

12.5 Who leads in the line of rikishi?

A gyoji of the same rank, one for each side. The gyoji doing this duty are rotated so that they all get an equal share; the pairs for leading the dohyo-iri are based on position in the gyoji ranks. The most senior gyoji of the division appear together on the same day, and so on down to the most recently promoted.

> Note: The custom of having a gyoji lead in the line of sekitori goes back only to 1973. Before that, the sekitori simply walked on by themselves. Having a gyoji lead in has given the dohyo-iri much more focus — not to mention better timing.

12.6 What happens in the juryo and makuuchi dohyo-iri?

1) Warned by the clacking of a yobidashi's clappers (ki), they put on their kesho-mawashi in good time and assemble at the entrance to the hanamichi during the last few bouts of the preceding division. They usually wear a cotton yukata so as not to catch cold. When their turn comes, they hand the yukata to an assistant, line up, and wait for the first sound of the public address system announcing their entry.

2) The announcing is done from memory by a gyoji in ordinary clothes sitting across from the hanamichi at the front side of the dohyo. He gives the shikona, birthplace, and heya. As a man's name is called, he moves forward. He gets his

timing from a yobidashi standing at the corner of the dohyo clacking his wooden blocks. One clack comes when the man starts moving forward, and the next is when he climbs up. As the last man is coming up, the clappers beat faster, heightening the excitement of the event.

Note: Strictly speaking the second item is where the family's official family register is kept, which may be quite different from the actual birthplace. Terao, for instance, was born in Tokyo because his father was an active rikishi there at the time; but he is still recorded as being from Kagoshima.

3) In a counter-clockwise direction they walk slowly around the outside of the straw circle until the first man reaches almost full circle and stands at the corner facing up the hanamichi from which he came. The next man stops behinds him and turns, facing outwards, and gradually a circle of standing men is formed.

4) As the last man gets up (usually the ozeki in the case of the makuuchi), they all turn facing inwards.

5) In unison they clap their hands once in front of their chests.

6) They raise their right hands in a greeting gesture.

7) Slipping the fingers of both hands under the side of their kesho mawashi just below the waist, they raise it a little and then drop it again.

8) They raise both hands together.

9) They descend from the dohyo and return to their changing room in the same order in which they entered, again to the accompaniment of clappers.

Note: The present form of dohyo-iri was laid down in 1973.

12.7 What is the meaning of the dohyo-iri?

It is a cut-down form of the dohyo-iri of the Edo period, when each circle of men performed a longer series of motions more like the yokozuna dohyo-iri of today. The small motions of today represent much larger ones of former years:

1) The single handclap represents the symbolic washing of the hands.

2) The raising of the right hand is all that remains of the highest part of the sandan-gamae.

3) The slight twitching of the top of the kesho-mawashi represents the shiko leg-raising and stomping.

4) The raising of both hands is the end of the shiko movement.

12.8 How does today's makuuchi dohyo-iri differ from that of the Edo period?

In the late Edo and early Meiji, there was more room because about ten men mounted the dohyo at once, so they performed a complete shiko with wide arm and leg movements, as we can see from the swirl of the kesho-mawashi in the prints of the period. It is not clearly known when the movements were so severely curtailed, although mid-Meiji has been suggested.

12.9 Did the participants always face outwards, toward the audience?

No, this was introduced in 1952. Before that, they faced into the ring.

12.10 When does the juryo dohyo-iri take place?

It is normally timed for about 2.45 except on the final day, when everything is half an hour early to allow for the prize-giving. Its place in the program is toward the end of the makushita bouts, when there are five bouts of that level remaining. After the dohyo-iri the final makushita bouts take place. This is for the practical reason that the men in the first of the juryo bouts need time to change out of their kesho-mawashi and into their shimekomi.

12.11 When does the makuuchi dohyo-iri take place?

At the end of the juryo bouts. It is normally timed for about 3:55 (except on the final day) but the bouts in juryo and below often overrun, if there are many long bouts or many instances of mono-ii, disputed decisions leading to judges' conferences. Since the 'facing outward' stance was introduced in 1952, there have been a number of modifications.

12.12 What happens when the Emperor or Crown Prince is present?

There is a special dohyo-iri, based on the rule that no-one should turn his back on these personages, so the ordinary dohyo-iri in which they all turn inwards cannot be performed.

Led by the gyoji, the rikishi stand in a long line in the hanamichi and slowly bow. Then they ascend the dohyo and stand in lines across the square top of the dohyo facing the Royal Box, the lowest-ranked at the front and the highest at the rear. When all the men on the east are lined up in rows, they perform a handclap and shiko, much like the men of the Edo period did; then go down into a sonkyo squat.

The gyoji in plain clothes sitting at the front announces each man by name, birthplace and heya as usual; but there are two differences: gyoji who has led in the line and has been squatting in the front corner, has his name called and takes a bow before leaving for the changing room. Then each man as his name is called bows and leaves, so the number constantly gets less. The other difference is that, in this case, the gyoji calling the names is allowed to carry them written on a piece of paper when he would otherwise call them from memory.

12.13 Can there be a dohyo-iri for makushita and below?

No; the right to parade in kesho-mawashi belongs only to sekitori.

12.14 How long has there been a dohyo-iri in sumo?

The oldest depictions on woodblock prints date back to the early 18th century, during a period that ran from 1716 to 1736. But at that time they paraded in their regular mawashi. A separate kesho-mawashi developed a little later, within the space of about 15 years from 1750.

12.15 What were the 'kanban ozeki' of the Edo period?

They were boys and men employed to perform a dohyo-iri and nothing else, as an attraction. They were mostly very tall or large men, and exceptionally big fat boys. Since they did no sumo at all, they were more of a freak show than a distinction; their function was simply to pull in the crowds. 'Kanban' is literally a shop's signboard or a billboard.

Section 2 YOKOZUNA DOHYO-IRI

12.16 When does the yokozuna dohyo-iri ' 横綱土俵入り ' take place?

Right after the makuuchi dohyo-iri.

12.17 Is the form always the same?

To judge from old pictures, there was some variety in olden times, depending on the individual's character and personality. It is only in the 20th century that the movements have become stylized; and even now each yokozuna manages to stamp his own personality upon the performance. It grew out of the general dohyo-iri, which, to judge from the woodblock prints, seems to have begun in the Kyoho 享保 era (1716-1736), with all the rikishi of the east or the west side performing shiko, the foot-stamping, together in a circle. Something close to the present-day yokozuna dohyo-iri began in the Kansei 寛政 era (1789-1800) with Tanikaze and Onogawa, who received licenses to perform individual ceremonies. The present-day makuuchi dohyo-iri dates from around mid-Meiji, but the greater numbers of makuuchi rikishi today have led to the dropping of the foot-stamping, except when the Emperor is present (see tenran-zumo 13.27). So the yokozuna dohyo-iri of today is a survival from the past.

12.18 Has it always had this name?

It has also been called 'kataya-iri' and 'dezu-iri.' The yokozuna license that tanikaze received in 1789 calls the ritual 'kataya-iri.' The more recent term 'dezu-iri' dates from around 1930. Nowadays only 'dohyo-iri' is accepted by the Sumo Kyokai.

12.19 When there is more than one yokozuna, is there an order in their dohyo-iri?

Yes, there is. They come in according to their rank on the banzuke, except that, as in all other matters, east goes first on the odd-numbered days and west goes first on the even-numbered days of a basho. If there are three or more yokozuna, they each perform their dohyo-iri, but alternating sides.

12.20 How many styles of dohyo-iri are there?

Just two: Unryu and Shiranui. You can tell at a glance which is which from the shape of the knot at the back of the tsuna, the great white hawser worn around the yokozuna's waist. The Unryu style has one large loop in the center, while the Shiranui style has two smaller loops, side by side. Apart from this, there is one small difference in the position of the hands during the seri-agari (slow rise) part of the dohyo-iri ritual.

12.21 What is the difference in the seri-agari?

In the Unryu style the left hand is placed against the lower ribs, and the right hand held out to the wide, a little below shoulder level; in the Shiranui style, both arms are stretched out low to the sides, and the body goes rather lower at the start of the movement. The effect is of a great bird rising in flight.

12.22 Who decides which style a new yokozuna will adopt?

The man himself and his stablemaster talk it over and decide. The Sumo Kyokai does not decide; and there is no particular tradition of some heya having one style rather than the other.

12.23 When did the Unryu and Shiranui styles begin?

It is not certain. The Shiranui style is supposed to resemble the dohyo-iri of the 11th yokozuna, Shiranui Koemon, and the Unryu, that of the 10th yokozuna, Unryu Hisakichi; but this has no foundation in fact. If you look at the woodblock prints of these men performing their dohyo-iri, the styles actually appear to be reversed though admittedly they are impressive. So we can say that they are simply names that recall dignified dohyo-iri of the 19th century.

Note: The two modern forms may be traced back to Umegatani II (Unryu) and Tachiyama (Shiranui); it was an observer with a bad memory who made the wrong attributions.

12.24 Is there a fixed form for the entry and exit?

There is. Led by the chief or deputy chief yobidashi beating his clappers, the yokozuna walks in preceded by the tsuyu-harai (dew-sweeper) and followed by his tachi-mochi (sword-bearer). The chief or deputy chief gyoji brings up the rear. The yobidashi crouches in the rear corner, and the gyoji takes his position at the center rear. The three rikishi climb up together from the east or west side, the yokozuna in the middle and the sword-bearer on his right and the dew-sweeper on his left.

12.25 Is there any qualification for the attendants?

The tachimochi 太刀持ち , who is always on the yokozuna's right hand, is senior to the tsuyu-harai. Both must be of makuuchi rank, and if the yokozuna's heya does not have two other men in the top division, other heya in the ichimon will be approached - or men may be invited as a favor from unrelated heya.

12.26 Is the sword real?

o **Tachi (sword)** 太刀

Akebono was at first given two apparent swords, but they were only fancy handles fitted into empty scabbards of Wajima lacquer, kin-nashi jinuri kirimon kin-makie (金梨　地塗桐紋　金蒔絵), in the Kamakura Muromachi style. In Kyushu 1994 he was finally using a real sword, presented to him by the Society for the Preservation of Japanese Art Swords. (The presentation was scheduled for summer but he was off from mid-basho in May, and all July and September.

The blade was made by Yoshiwara Yoshindo, considered near the top of the 300-odd present-day swordsmiths excluding two Living Treasures and represents about one month's work. The work was more difficult because the blade had to fit an existing scabbard, whereas the blade is usually made first and the scabbard made to fit it. This sword was polished by Fujishiro Okisato (again, taking several weeks).

12.27 How much does the sword weigh?

It depends on the yokozuna; in general, his sword and his tsuna are in proportion.

Akebono's sword weighs 1.6 kg., and is one meter long, in keeping with his size; Chiyonofuji's, by contrast, was 10 cm. shorter.

12.28 What is the white rope belt?

o **Tsuna** 綱、横綱

The great white hawser is renewed three times a year, on a taian (auspicious) day before the Tokyo basho. Akebono's weighed 22 kg. Takanohana's first weighed a mere 15 kg., and was 4 meters long; it took 30 minutes to make. Akebono's first was so badly made (he was that heya's first sekitori, let alone yokozuna) that they had to discard it and start again.

The strips of folded white paper tucked into the front of the tsuna are commonly called shide 紙垂 , not gohei 御幣 (the old term). There are always five of them, each folded into four. In the 19th century, shide were cut and folded in different ways.

12.29 Is the tsuna ready-made?

No, it has to be coiled and knotted each time it is worn.

Equipment needed for putting on the tsuna

white cotton gloves
wire cutters (bansen) (for trimming the wire ends)
white paper tape and talcum powder (for masking minor scuffs)
soft brush (for cleaning sand off kesho-mawashi)
screwdriver with tape covering end (for inserting shide)
scissors (for cutting tape, trimming ends)
wooden tablet (no longer used but still part of the kit!)

12.30 Is it possible for a yokozuna to perform the dohyo-iri after his retirement?

Yes, it is, if the Kyokai considers it necessary. For instance, although Wakanohana III announced his retirement on Day 5 of the March tournament in the year 2000, he appeared at the Ise Shrine and for the rest of the tour in April. His popularity ensured good attendances and better ticket sales. On a previous occasion, the recently-retired Hokutoumi performed the dohyo-iri on an overseas exhibition tour in 1992 as there was no active yokozuna at that time. And in 1974, both Kitanofuji and Kotozakura performed in the summer tour. More recently, Takanohana performed at Takatoriki's retirement and on several other occasions before his ceremonial haircut.

12.31 What are the yokozuna's movements in the dohyo-iri?

1) Enters preceded by yobidashi with clappers, tsuyu-harai (露払い, dew-sweeper) and tachimochi 太刀持ち, sword-bearer) and followed by the officiating gyoji. Normally the tate-gyoji Kimura Shonosuke comes on whichever side, east or west, takes precedence that day, and the other tate-gyoji Shikimori Inosuke escorts the yokozuna of the other side. The tate-yobidashi and fuku-tate-yobidashi usually reverse the order.

2) Mounts dohyo on east or west side together with the sword-bearer on his right and the dew-sweeper on his left. The two attendants go down into a squat which they must maintain like statues for the whole of the time. The gyoji takes a position center back and goes into a squat.

3) Sonkyo:
With legs bent out sideways and the torso upright, he claps his hands twice (to attract the attention of the divinities), cups his hands upwards and moves them out and up. Alternative forms are: the hands just meet above the head, with the arms rounded (notably Taiho's style); or the upper arms are out to the sides and the forearms up at right angles.

4) Chiri-chozu:
The arms go out and round, the hands coming together in front of the chest for the chiri-chozu, cutting the dust: the hands flat together pointing forward , then

the fingers of the left hand move up and over slightly; then the palms are rubbed together in a 'washing' motion. This is an old samurai custom: before battle, the hands were washed if possible; but in the field there was not always water, so grasses were picked and rubbed between the hands. If the terrain was so bare that there was no grass, the warriors still went through the motions so that their hands were rubbed clean. Oddly enough, a tea ceremony begins with the exact same movement.

5) The arms go out again and up over the head, then into a slow circular outward movement; they hesitate at shoulder level, then quickly move down into a kashiwade, 拍 手 , literally oak-hand, a hand-clap, but with the hands pointed forward not up. The hands go out again at shoulder level, the palms face front then quickly turn down.

Note: All of 4 and 5 are called chiri o kiru, cutting the dust or dirt.

6) The yokozuna rises, adjusts his kesho-mawashi, walks to the center of the ring, turns and faces front. The gyoji, who has been standing about a third of the way into the circle, moves back to the rear and goes into a squat, and prepares to give the keihitsu, a clearly-audible exhalation that accompanies the yokozuna's next movements.

7) With legs astride, the yokozuna repeats the hand movements of 3, 4 and 5.

8) Shiko:
With the left hand cupped under the breast, the right hand goes up high to the side (palm front, then downwards); then the hands reverse as the weight goes onto the left leg. Balancing on his left leg, and with his left hand on that knee, the yokozuna lifts his right foot as high as he can to the side, then brings it down firmly on the ground, his right hand slapping his thigh as it comes down.

9) Seri-agari:

Unryu style: with the left hand on the lower ribs, and the right hand out to the wide, a little below shoulder level, the yokozuna squats with his knees out to the sides, if possible, forming a perfect rectangle with the ground, and then making small 'swimming' motions with his feet along the white paint lines, he slowly moves about a meter forward, while his torso slowly comes upright.

Shiranui style: the only difference is in the position of the hands and arms at the beginning of the seri-agari: both arms are stretched out low to the sides, and the body goes rather lower at the start of the movement. The effect is of a great bird rising in flight.

10) With the right hand bent to the side, and the left hand out above the shoulder, the arms drop, and the man performs shiko (as 8); first the right leg, then the left, each ending with both hands pressing the legs down into a crouch.

11) With the hands on each side of the kesho-mawashi to keep it straight, the yokozuna rises, returns to his original place on the east (or west) side, repeats movements (3) to (5), and, holding the kesho-mawashi steady, rises and walks out with his attendants and the chief gyoji in the same order as they came in.

Section 3 YUMITORI-SHIKI

12.32 What is the bow ceremony?

Coming immediately after the musubi no ichiban, the last bout, it is the final event of every public sumo performance. It represents the triumph of the winner of the final bout, and by extension, of all those who have won that day. Formerly it took place only on the final day, but since March 1952 it has been done every day as part of the spectacle. The literal meaning of the name is 'bow-taking ceremony,' and it is also commonly referred to as 'bow-twirling ceremony' and 'bow-brandishing ceremony.'

12.33 Who performs the bow ceremony?

In principle, it is a man of makushita rank who belongs to a heya that has a yokozuna in it. He is selected as a result of consultations between the stablemaster, the yokozuna himself, and such people as the wakaimono-gashira.

12.34 Is the performer always a makushita?

There have been cases where a man was demoted to sandanme and even jonidan but retained the job; there have also been cases where a man was promoted to juryo and kept doing the ceremony for a time.

12.35 Must he be an active rikishi?

Certainly. He must train and fight regular bouts like his fellows, and do other duties appropriate to his rank; this is simply an extra job, for which he receives a fee.

12.36 Why does he have a kesho mawashi and an o-icho hairstyle?

He is dressed like a sekitori because he is representing a yokozuna on the dohyo. It is possible that having the appearance of a rank above his own is the origin of the superstition that men who perform the yumitori-shiki do not get promoted to sekitori. In fact, several men have broken this superstition.

12.37 What happens if he drops the bow on the dohyo?

Despite the difficulty of the rapid twirling motion, this is a very uncommon occurrence; but there is a superstition that he must not put his hand on the dohyo, so he steps on the bow sharply with one foot until it bounces up high enough for him to catch hold of it again.

12.38 What happens if he drops the bow below the dohyo?

A yobidashi runs round to pick it up and hand it up to him. While he is waiting, the performer must do shiko, the sideways leg-lifts and foot stamps.

12.39 When does he come in and where does he wait?

When all eyes are on the contestants in the final bout, who have received the water of power and are just starting their shikiri, he moves down the hanamichi unobtrusively and takes his seat between the two judges at the rear, beside the tate gyoji (Shikimori Inosuke) who has just finished officiating and has returned to the gyoji tamari.

The reason for tsitting in the middle is that, as he will represent the winner, he has to wait until the bout is decided. Then he moves round to the side of the winner and climbs onto the dohyo by the step from which the victor has just climbed down.

12.40 Does he carry the bow with him down the hanamichi?

No; a yobidashi holds the bow until the performer is on the dohyo, then hands it to the chief gyoji to pass over. At the end of the ceremony the bow is returned to the chief gyoji who passes it back to the yobidashi.

UNIT 13   PROMOTION AND DEMOTION AT THE TOP

Section 1   OZEKI

13.1 What are the qualifications for promotion to ozeki?

They are deliberately left a little vague, because at this level there are several factors to be taken into account besides simple arithmetic. The basic factor is the aggregate total of wins over the last three basho. Since 1986 no sekiwake has been promoted with an aggregate of less than 32 wins, and most new ozeki have scored 34 or 35. But the quality of the opposition, and the way of winning, are also taken into account. Tricky sumo is not considered befitting; and if many men were absent in the yokozuna and ozeki ranks and therefore the man did not have a chance to meet (and presumably beat) them, his chances might be less. There have also been cases in the past where a man had managed a score as good as others who had been promoted — but the Kyokai considered that there were already enough ozeki. This happened to Hasegawa, who won a yusho at sekiwake in March 1972. (Although his aggregate was only 30-15, his previous 3 scores were 8-7, 10-5, and 12-3, winning in a playoff.)

13.2 What advantages does an ozeki have?

Unlike every rank below him, he is not demoted for a single losing score; but if he has two make-koshi in a row, then he is said to be kadoban (roughly, at the turning point) and if he gets a third makekoshi, then he is demoted to sekiwake. He has a further cushion, however; if he gets ten or more wins in this position, he automatically returns to his ozeki rank. (This was brought in in July 1969.) If not, then he must start all over again trying to qualify for a second promotion to ozeki.

The ozeki has a further advantage at retirement: if he has not obtained a myoseki that entitles him to remain in the Kyokai as one of its elders, he can be a sort of honorary elder under his professional name for three years (yokozuna have the same privilege for five years). This is not to be confused with the ichidai toshiyori system (14.7) or the jun-toshiyori (14.9) system.

13.3 What is the Ozeki-kai?

An association of past and present ozeki that meets socially once a year on Day 3 of the Fukuoka Basho in November.

Section 2 YOKOZUNA

13.4 What are the qualifications for promotion to yokozuna?

That's even more vague than for ozeki promotion, since the question of upholding the dignity of the position also arises. This is not simply the top rank in sumo, but a symbol of Japanese cultural values. But one widely-accepted rule is that the man should have won two consecutive yusho and, of course, already be at the ozeki rank at least when winning the second championship.

13.5 If sumo has been going on for so many centuries, why are there fewer than 70 yokozuna?

That's a very good question. The short answer is that, for most of sumo's history, neither the name nor the rank existed.

Note: As of February 2022, yokozuna Terunofuji is the 73rd.

13.6 Who was the first yokozuna?

The first clear record of men being granted permission to wear the tsuna or yokozuna (that is, the white twisted belt) and perform a separate dohyo-iri is in 1789, when Tanikaze received a license from the Yoshida Tsukasa family of Kumamoto, southern Japan, in November, and his rival Onogawa a month later in December.

When the list was being made up in the late 19th century, however, it was thought that three men of earlier times were famous enough to be retrospectively included, even though their careers were not clearly recorded and the earliest, Akashi, was an almost legendary figure of the early 17th century about whom little is known. So Akashi, Ayagawa (whose dates of birth and death are not known) and Maruyama, who definitely wore the tsuna but who is not recorded as having been licensed, became the first three on the all-time list of yokozuna, and leaving Tanikaze and Onogawa as numbers 4 and 5.

13.7 Who produced the list of yokozuna that gives them their numbers?

This was the elder Jinmaku, who attempted in 1895 to compile a chronological list of all the yokozuna. The task was formidable, and when Jinmaku published his proposed list in 1900 it was immediately attacked as unreliable. Controversy raged for years, until the Kyokai finally declared it official in 1926 — apparently to put an end to the arguments rather than from any conviction that it was correct.

13.8 So what are the real facts about yokozuna?

They started off as ozeki who were permitted to perform an individual dohyo-iri instead of in the group of all the east side or all the west side men. In November 1789, a man called Yoshida Tsukasa, who was trying to claim ascendancy over the sumo authorities, 'granted' licenses to perform yokozuna dohyo-iri to two famous ozeki, Tanikaze (1750-95) and Onogawa (1758-1806).

Note: Tanikaze and Onogawa both were listed as sekiwake in the banzuke of November 1791, but were considered true ozeki. The two ozeki listed on that banzuke, Kumonryu and Tsukushigata, were added as especially uncommon rikishi who would attract customers.

13.9 Does the Yoshida family still issue certificates?

No; since 1951 the Nihon Sumo Kyokai has put itself in charge of licensing yokozuna.

13.10 Who was the first 'real' yokozuna?

Nishinoumi was officially listed on the banzuke as a yokozuna in May 1890 — the first time the word appeared there. It was done simply to avoid an awkward situation. In May 1890 there were four men at the rank of ozeki, and in the previous basho Nishinoumi's record had been the worst of the four, so his name was to be put into the least prestigious position. He grumbled, 'I've got a yokozuna license — what's the meaning of putting my name out at the side?' and to satisfy him, 'yokozuna' was put on the banzuke.

But this was still only a title given to an ozeki. It was not until February 1909 (when a number of new rules and customs were formalized, taking advantage of the opening of the first Kokugikan), that the Kyokai officially defined yokozuna as a separate rank above ozeki.

13.11 How does a man become a yokozuna?

To put it simply, he must be an ozeki who subsequently receives the unanimous approval of the rijikai, the Board of Directors of the Sumo Association. The criteria are, however, deliberately left somewhat blurred because this is not merely sumo's highest rank: as sumo itself is more than a sport, so a yokozuna is supposed to embody the spirit and dignity of sumo as well as being able to beat all comers.

There is a general guideline that has in recent years been firmly insisted upon: that an ozeki should win two championships in succession, 'or equivalent' — a qualification that is usually taken as meaning close runner-up, in particularhaving been beaten in a play-off. Takanohana's promotion was held back for some time because, although he had already won more championships than some other men who had been promoted, he won all the Tokyo basho but none of the provincial tournaments in between. Finally he overcame this jinx and won the all-important back-to-back yusho and clinched his promotion. In contrast, his elder brother Wakanohana got two successive yusho in 1998 and was forthwith promoted although he had a much less distinguished overall record.

To allow some leeway, there are two intangibles added to the guidelines: 'hinkaku' and 'rikiryô.' 'Rikiryo' may be translated as 'power' or 'overwhelming ability.' 'Hinkaku,' however, is harder to define. 'Dignity' is the closest; but really it refers to that overwhelming presence possessed by a true yokozuna. So it is easy to criticize an ozeki for not having it, even when he has fulfilled all the other criteria.

13.12 Does the rijikai have sole responsibility to decide the promotion?

No; in 1950 an advisory body, the yokozuna shingi-iinkai, the Yokozuna Deliberation Council, was set up.

13.13 What is the Yokozuna Deliberation Council?

It is an advisory body set up by the Sumo Kyokai. It consists of up to 15 members, appointed by the Kyokai from the general public and not the sumo world; all must have a long-standing interest in sumo and be well-informed about it. After years of half-promises and delays, finally one woman was appointed to it.

13.14 When does the Council meet?

1) About ten days before a Tokyo basho begins, the members (and the press and many invited guests) attend the keiko soken, a (semi) public training session for the title-holders and the upper makushita. It is held in the kyoshujo, the sumo training school within the Kokugikan (1.21). This session provides the Council, the upper officials of the Kyokai, and the press with a chance to see the condition of the top men. If an ozeki or yokozuna candidate is in view, he will be the focus of attention. Since 2000, in May the Soken has been held in the Kokugikan itself and open to the general public.

2) On one day of a Tokyo basho, the Council members sit together in the audience to watch the sumo.

3) The Council meets after every basho, on the day after senshuraku, to discuss the performance of yokozuna and possible candidates.

13.15 How does the Yokozuna Deliberation Council operate?

The Sumo Association (actually the Rijicho, Chairman) asks it to consider a case when an ozeki is close to qualifying or has qualified for consideration. It holds a meeting on the day after each hon-basho ends, whether or not a promotion is close.

In January 1958 the following criteria were defined:

1) To be recommended for yokozuna promotion a man must have outstanding dignity and ability (see 13.1 above)

2) In principle it must be an ozeki who has won two successive championships.

3) In recommending promotion for a man with a record considered 'equivalent' to two championships, originally a unanimous decision was required; this has now been relaxed to a two-thirds majority.

13.16 Does the Council have any other duties?

Yes. Since 1958, it has been empowered to examine the performance of any existing yokozuna: by a two-thirds majority it can urge a yokozuna to perform better, give him a warning, even recommend that he retire. The following aspects of a yokozuna's performance are examined:

1) If he has had many absences. But even if he has been off sick for a long time, consideration is given to the reason (injury, illness) and to the likelihood of his being able to return to active competition. Since a yokozuna cannot be demoted, it is not fair to hurry him into retirement.

2) If his conduct is scandalous and unbefitting a yokozuna.

3) If he appears on the dohyo but his scores are consistently low for his high rank.

13.17 Is the Council's decision on yokozuna promotion final?

In practice, it appears to be; although technically the Kyokai has the final say. After the Council has delivered its recommendation, the rijikai meets and comes to its decision. The matter then goes to the banzuke hensei kaigi, the regular meeting that arranges the order of names in the banzuke for the following hon-basho. This is three days after the last day of the basho just finished. It is at this meeting that the yokozuna's promotion is formally decided — since it is now agreed that his name will be entered in the yokozuna rank on the next banzuke.

13.18 How is the new yokozuna informed of his promotion?

After the banzuke meeting, two representatives of the Kyokai — one riji (director) and one judge — go to the man's heya, where the stablemaster, his wife, and the promotee are waiting in formal Japanese dress. Sitting on large cushions, in front of a barrage of microphones and surrounded by press photographers, the two messengers face the new yokozuna and announce the Kyokai's decision. This is called 'yokozuna dentatsu-shiki' — the Yokozuna Notification Ceremony.

13.19 What is said at this ceremony?

Something like this: 'I hereby inform you that today, the banzuke hensei kaigi and the rijikai unanimously decided that ozeki XYZ should be promoted to yokozuna.'

The new yokozuna replies, 'tsutsushinde o-uke shimasu.' — 'I humbly accept, and will strive to uphold the honor of the name of yokozuna.' Each man will try to say something a little different, since his words will be memorialized, but basically the meaning is the same. Since the ozeki promotion is announced in exactly the same way, the man has had at least one chance to do it before!

13.20 From when is he counted a yokozuna?

From the day on which his name is accepted at the banzuke meeting. The same applies to a new ozeki. But in the case of a new juryo promotion, although the man is informed, with less ceremony, on the same day, he does not count as a juryo until the banzuke is published 13 days before the next basho. The early warning is for the practical purpose of giving him time to order his silk shimekomi and kesho-mawashi. (Unit 2, section 3, 4)

13.21 If two new yokozuna are promoted at the same time, how is the order decided?

Every yokozuna is numbered in order from the rather hazy first; but in this rare case, the order is not decided until one retires, in which case he is earlier on the list and the remaining man follows him.

13.22 What advantages does a yokozuna have?

Unlike all other rikishi, he cannot be demoted for a poor showing; but this is not necessarily an advantage because if he fails to maintain a consistently good standard he may come under pressure from the Yokoshin and the Kyokai to retire; whereas a demoted ozeki may regain his abilities and make a successful comeback, a yokozuna may have to retire early. On retirement, however, he has a full five years within which he can be an elder of the Kyokai under his own name while he tries to obtain title to a myoseki. In fact yokozuna in this position have always succeeded in buying a myoseki within the five years.

13.23 What are the two styles of yokozuna?

They differ only in some aspects of the dohyo-iri ring-entering ceremony. There are two styles, Unryu (the more common) and Shiranui, and they are supposed to represent the particularly impressive dohyo-iri performed by two famous yokozuna of the old days. Oddly enough, the naming of the two styles seems to have been done by someone with a poor memory;some old woodblock prints were found which revealed that the original Unryu performed in the Shiranui style and vice versa.The tsuna is tied in one big loop at the back for the Unryu style, while the Shiranui style had two loops like wings. In the actual performance, the only variation is in the position of the hands and arms during the seri-agari, the slow inching forward movement as the man rises from a crouch to full height. In the Unryu style the right hand is raised high to the side while the left hand is placed on the chest at lower rib level. By contrast, the Shiranui style yokozuna begins the seri-agari with both hands out low at the aside and gradually raises them.

Section 3 TSUNA-UCHI — Making the tsuna

13.24 Where does the new yokozuna's tsuna come from?

It is made in the tsuna-uchi ceremony for which preparations start as soon as his promotion is announced. In fact every yokozuna has his tsuna remade three times a year, just before the Tokyo basho; but it is only the first time that is a great celebration.

13.25 Where is the tsuna made?

In his own heya. All the rikishi of his heya and the other heya in the same ichimon come to help — or at least, to be present. Another yokozuna, for instance, will not join in the physical work, but will sit watching, to honor the occasion with his presence.

13.26 How is the tsuna made?

The training area is covered with clean tarpaulins. Three lengths of pure white cotton fabric are spread out on the ground and copper wires of the same length are laid along them. Wrapped around the wires are hemp fibers, softened to a woolly texture, to pad out the tsuna. There is a lot of padding in the middle and gradually less towards the ends of each strand.

The three strands are rolled up into very long sausage shapes, and one end of each is tied to the teppo pole that is found in every heya's training area. Then the twisting begins. The rikishi, with their cotton mawashi covered with a strip of white cloth and with twisted headbands of celebratory red-and-white cotton on their heads, begin passing the three strands from hand to hand, right over left and under, all the time pulling to keep the tension correct. One rikishi sits underneath and pulls at the tsuna to make sure that it is kept straight. To make sure that his hair oil does not soil the pure white cotton cover of the tsuna, his head is covered with a white cloth worn like a scarf. The atmosphere is cheerful and noisy, with the shouts of the rikishi counting 'One, two, three!' and the sound of somebody beating a drum — or even a large tin can — to keep time. They work in shifts, as the work is hard and everybody has to take a turn.

At last the whole tsuna is finished. The pulling and twisting are all that hold it together; the three strands are not tied together in any way. Finally the shide are put in. Shide, also called gohei, are the five strips of pure white paper folded into zigzags that hang down the front of the yokozuna's keshô-mawashi looking like lightning flashes. The new yokozuna's senior tsukebito takes an instrument a little like a paper knife and pries the strands of the tsuna apart at the front just enough to slip in the top ends of the five shide.

The whole thing is coiled, laid on a cushion for all to admire (and all the important supporters to have their picture taken with) while the new yokozuna and his two makuuchi attendants put on old kesho-mawashi ready for his lesson in the dohyo-iri, which follows immediately. A retired yokozuna takes him through the movements and he practises as many times as necessary, until he feels sure of himself.

On the next day, or at most the day after, he will give his first public dohyo-iri in the forecourt of the Meiji Shrine, after first receiving his certificate and the tsuna, which has been blessed in the shrine.

13.27 How old is the yokozuna dohyo-iri? 横綱土俵入り

Judging from the woodblock prints, a general dohyo-iri seems to have begun in the Kyoho 享 保 era (1716-1736), with the rikishi performing shiko, the foot-stamping, in a circle. Something close to the present-day yokozuna dohyo-iri began in the Kansei 寛 政 era (1789-1800) with Tanikaze and Onogawa. The present-day makuuchi dohyo-iri dates from around mid-Meiji, but the greater numbers of makuuchi rikishi today have led to the dropping of the foot-stamping, except when the Emperor is present (see Tenran-zumo 12.17).

UNIT 14 RETIREMENT AND DANPATSU-SHIKI

Section 1 RETIREMENT

14.1 Who decides when it is time for a rikishi to retire?

Usually the man himself has a talk with his stablemaster and decides. Sometimes, however, the master urges him to keep trying for a little longer; conversely, sometimes the master urges him to quit and the rikishi decides to continue. When the decision is made, they deliver a notice of retirement to the Kyokai, and immediately after, hold a press conference. Then the most important supporters must be informed without delay, and preparations begun for the retirement ceremony. It occasionally happens that a master may unilaterally deliver notice of a man's retirement when there is a serious problem between them. This happened, for instance, in the case of the unsuccessful yokozuna Futahaguro, who was 'retired' in this way; in this case there is no appeal.

14.2 What choices are open to a man when he retires?

If he qualifies, he may stay on in the Sumo Association in one of a small number of capacities; otherwise, he must quit the world of sumo and become a private citizen. Very many men in the latter category, which is by far the most numerous, remain in some kind of sumo-related business, running a restaurant or bar, for instance.

14.3 What are the Kyokai jobs a retiree can do?

The best is to become a toshiyori, also called oyakata (elder); failing to qualify for this, a small number of men can become wakaimono-gashira (eight positions) or sewanin (also eight positions). Lower-ranking men may be hired in some capacity by a stablemaster, as heya 'managers' for instance; but this is a private arrangement and they are not members of the Kyokai.

14.4 Are 'toshiyori' and 'oyakata' the same?

Both mean 'elder' in English. Strictly speaking, 'toshiyori' refers to the status or position, while 'oyakata' is the title of respect given to a toshiyori. A toshiyori is a man who has acquired a toshiyori myoseki, one of the official positions in the Sumo Kyokai. It is also called a kabu, literally stock or share, although the sumo people feel that this has too commercial a sound. Each myoseki bears a name which was originally the name of a famous rikishi of the Edo or Meiji period.

14.5 How does a man become a toshiyori?

When a sekitori is ready to retire, he shows proof of possession of a myoseki, and the rijikai gives him a certificate called toshiyori myosekisho. His new name is then entered on the Kyokai's roll, and from now on he will be engaged in work for the Kyokai and will receive a salary according to his status.

14.6 How many myoseki are there?

The number is fixed at 105.

14.7 Then how is it that there are more than 105 toshiyori?

1) An outstanding yokozuna may be given the privilege of being an ichidai toshiyori, a single-generation elder. This means that he has the status of a toshiyori, with its privileges and duties, without having to own a myoseki. He

retains his famous professional name, shikona, and can run a heya with that name. He cannot, however, pass it on to a successor, since he has no myoseki to sell. This system was introduced in 1965. So far only three great yokozuna have become such ichidai toshiyori: Taiho, Kitanoumi and Takanohana. The honor was offered to Chiyonofuji too, but he declined it, preferring the prospect of taking over the prestigious Kokonoe myoseki and keeping the option of seeing his shikona bestowed upon a famous man of later times.

2) Any yokozuna who retires without a myoseki has the privilege of continuing for five years as an oyakata with his own shikona — in effect, in the same way as an ichidai-toshiyori. If he fails to acquire the rights to a myoseki at the end of that time, however, he must quit sumo. This has never so far happened.

14.8 What are the qualifications for holding a myoseki?

The requirements were changed in 1998. Formerly a man needed only one basho in makuuchi, or twenty consecutive basho in juryo, or a total of 26 basho in juryo. In 1998, however, the Kyokai tightened the requirements considerably in an effort to reduce the fierce competition for myôseki that was escalating the price.

They are now:

1) yokozuna or ozeki
2) one complete basho in sanyaku
3) 20 basho or more in makuuchi
4) 30 basho or more in juryo or juryo and makuuchi
5) a person who inherits a heya and who has served at least 12 basho in makuuchi, or at least 20 basho in juryo, or juryo and makuuchi

14.9 Must a man buy a myoseki outright?

It has often happened in the past that a successful man who had acquired the rights to a myoseki while he was still active rented out his myoseki to a man who had none. The only formality was to present a statement to the Kyokai stamped with the personal seals of both men. The payments helped the myoseki's owner to finish paying off the loan he had taken out to buy it. It was also common for a stablemaster to hold several spare myoseki which he could use as incentives to recruit promising men.

But there have been considerable changes in the 1990s and early 2000s, and matters have not yet settled down. In May 1998 some severe changes were brought in, including: owning more than one myoseki would be forbidden; the renting of myoseki would be banned, though men already renting one would be allowed up to five years to find one available for purchase; and to ease the pressure which would be caused by these restrictions, ten jun-toshiyori (associate elder) positions would be established, whereby a man who was qualified to hold a myoseki but had not got one could remain as an elder under his own shikona for up to two years. (This was similar to the existing privilege of five years for a yokozuna and three years for an ozeki).

In September 2002, however, the Kyokai was running short of toshiyori available to carry out its work, and announced some modifications: the renting of myoseki would again be allowed, but the name of the real owner would be publicly announced. The holding of multiple myoseki would still be banned, the number of jun-toshiyori positions would be reduced from ten to five, and the time limit from two years to one.

14.10 Can a non-Japanese become a toshiyori?

No. At the moment of announcing his retirement, a rikishi must have Japanese citizenship. Therefore, if a foreign-born rikishi intends to remain in the world of sumo, he needs to apply for naturalization well before he is likely to retire. This nationality clause was introduced in 1976, at a time when Hawaiian-born Takamiyama and the Japanese-Korean Kaneshiro looked as if they would qualify. Before that, the question had never arisen. In the event, Takamiyama took Japanese nationality and on retirement became Azumazeki oyakata, while Kaneshiro developed health problems and quit sumo without attempting to acquire a myoseki.

14.11 Can a myoseki be passed on to someone outside sumo?

No, it cannot be transferred to a person not qualified to hold it. Nor can it be offered as security for a loan — a transgression that brought about the downfall of the former great yokozuna Wajima, who used his Hanakago myoseki in that way. The Kyokai responded by confiscating it and passing it on to a man of their own choice. On the other hand, the widow of an oyakata is not obliged to transfer his myoseki immediately, but can keep it, sometimes for years, until she decides on a suitable successor.

14.12 What is a danpatsu-shiki?

It is the ceremonial cutting off of the mage (topknot) which only rikishi are allowed to wear.

14.13 What does the danpatsu represent?

It is called 'danpatsu' rather than 'sanpatsu ' (the ordinary word for a haircut) because of its finality. It marks the end of one life and the beginning of another.

14.14 What is the qualification for having a danpatsu-shiki in the Kokugikan?

According to the Rikishikai (Association of Rikishi), the man must have been at sekitori level for at least thirty basho.

14.15 What happens at a danpatsu-shiki?

The retiree, in effect, rents the Kokugikan for the day and sells as many tickets as possible to his supporters and the general public, in the hope of garnering a profit that will cushion his retirement. A very popular man, like Chiyonofuji, may achieve a sell-out, whereas most men sell all the downstairs seats but only a few of the seats in the balcony. In recent years there have even been cases of less well-connected men who, while insisting on their privilege of having a haircut in the arena, made no attempt to sell tickets but limited the event to their own friends and supporters.

While the basic form is always the same, the retiree and his sponsors try to find something a little different and memorable. The doors open at 11:00 a.m., when the retiree and all the sekitori of his ichimon, plus personal friends from other ichimon, show themselves in the entrance hall in formal kimono. This is an opportunity to get autographs and photos, though the crowd makes either difficult. On the dohyo, between about noon and 4:00 p.m. when the event ends, there will be such events as a knockout contest for the makushita-ranking rikishi of the ichimon, a demonstration of drumming by a yobidashi, singing of jinku (sumo songs), a demonstration by a tokoyama of how to dress hair into a gingko-leaf style, shokkiri (comic sumo), a demonstration of putting on the yokozuna's white belt, juryo dohyo-iri and bouts, makuuchi and yokozuna dohyo-iri and bouts and somewhere in the middle, the ceremonial hair-cutting that represents the moment of retirement. In recent years the order has been varied with serious sumo alternating with light entertainment. In the bouts, the only difference from hon-basho sumo is that there are only two judges (east and west) instead of five; the warm-up time is shorter, and the rikishi tend not to take risks in order to win. The pairings are decided, not by the regular judging committee, but by the gyoji of the ichimon.

14.16 How is the hair cut?

The man sits on a chair near the front of the dohyo, with a senior gyoji standing on his right holding a plain Shinto-style wooden offering tray on which are placed a sheet of clean white paper and a pair of large gold-plated scissors. Male supporters, usually more than 140 and sometimes 300 or more, step up one by one onto the dohyo (in slippers) and standing behind him, take the scissors and snip just two or three hairs at the widest part of the hair below the mage. The gyoji often advises them where to cut. At the end, various sumo people come and take a cut: representatives of the Kyokai including the Chairman, the rikishikai and the ichimon. There is a flutter of excitement when still-active rikishi come up to take a snip wearing their silk shimekomi ready for the sumo.

14.17 Who makes the final cut?

The final cut (tome-basami) is made by the stablemaster (shisho) who carefully cuts around the base of the mage and severs it completely. He holds it aloft, and then the two of them bow to the four sides of the audience. After standing alone and hearing an announcer's voice narrating highlights of his career, the man retires to the dressing room where a real hairdresser, not a tokoyama, is waiting to give him his first modern hairstyle.

14.18 Do the supporters keep the hair?

No; they do not remove any hair. They are simply making a single snip in the wide area between the scalp and the string that binds the mage. That is, they are gradually loosening the mage from the hair nearer the scalp. If a man tries to remove a piece of hair as a souvenir, by taking two snips, it is considered bad manners.

14.19 When a yokozuna retires, does he perform a dohyo-iri?

Yes; it is a most impressive occasion, ideally with three yokozuna in a row. If possible he should be flanked by still-active yokozuna as his tachi-mochi and tsuyu-harai. If there is only one other yokozuna, the tsuyu-harai may be a makushita rikishi from the ichimon; but there is no rule, and an ozeki or a yokozuna from a different ichimon may appear to honor the retiree.

14.20 Do non-sekitori have a danpatsu-shiki too?

Yes, but not in the Kokugikan arena. If a man has had a long career but without qualifying for the Kokugikan, his supporters or his stablemaster may hire a hall in a hotel. Alternatively, the large hall in the basement of the Kokugikan may be rented. For a lower-ranker, a simple ceremony in the heya, attended only by his fellow-rikishi, his family and friends, may be all. But the cutting off of the mage is the same.

14.21 What is the difference between 'intai' and 'haigyo'?

Until recently the difference was that sekitori who were about to become oyakata used the word 'intai' (retirement), whilst all others were classified as 'haigyo' — quitting the business. The turning point came when the popular and successful

Kyokudozan chose to leave sumo and stand for election to Japan's House of Representatives. He won his seat, and it was felt that his departure from sumo could hardly be dismissed by the brusque and undignified 'haigyo,' so it was soon announced that henceforth voluntarily quitting sumo after a respectable career, whether the man would remain with the Sumo Association or not, would be 'intai.' 'Haigyo' is now used of men who have been in sumo a short time only, or who have had an unsuccessful career. Naturally, in cases of dismissal, disgrace, or running away, 'haigyo' is also used.

14.22 Can a man return to sumo after retiring?

No. Once his name has been removed from the Kyokai's list, he cannot return. This is why a master will sometimes delay handing in notice of retirement in the case of a rikishi who has dropped off the bottom of the banzuke though injury or sickness — or in the case of a foreigner who has run away but might come back!

Section 2   OYAKATA AND SUMO-BEYA

14.23 Can any oyakata set up a sumo-beya?

In theory, yes. It is, however, an expensive undertaking, and to obtain permission, the oyakata has to prove to the rijikai's satisfaction that he has the means to do it. For this he needs proof of having purchased the necessary plot of land, and a guarantee of enough money to build a heya on it. This is why only about half the toshiyori are heya-mochi oyakata (oyakata owning heya), while the other half are heya-tsuki oyakata (oyakata affiliated with heya).

14.24 Is it necessary to get permission from anyone else?

Yes. Before an oyakata can split off from the heya to which he is affiliated, he must get written permission from his shisho (stablemaster).

14.25 Is there any limit to the number of sumo-beya?

No. There is, however, a growing sense that there are now too many, as fewer boys are joining as apprentices, and at the time of writing there is ongoing discussion about how to limit the formation of new heya in future. It has even been suggested that only former yokozuna or ozeki should be allowed to set up a new heya, but this was greeted with derision, since an outstandingly talented practitioner is by no means always a successful teacher.

14.26 Does an oyakata need anything besides a building to start a heya?

The building is supposed to include a keikoba (training area), and the oyakata must have recruited at least two apprentices. Formerly only one was needed, and sometimes in the past a man has started a heya with his own son as his sole deshi. In some cases, too, the heya is a private dwelling without a keikoba.

14.27 Does a stablemaster receive any money from the Kyokai?

Yes, the Kyokai pays support money according to the number of rikishi, but the figures are not made public. The amount is also said to be larger for the Tokyo basho than the others. There are also specific allowances intended to provide a heya with a keikoba, baths and anything else needed to ensure proper training.

14.28 Does a heya receive any money from the Kyokai for junior rikishi?

Yes; although they do not get a salary from the Kyokai, a master receives ¥65,000 for each rikishi in the lower ranks (makushita and below), to help him train them.

14.29 What does the Kyokai pay a stablemaster for his sekitori?

Because a master is credited with the success of his deshi, he receives a higher allowance for the more successful ones, on a sliding scale. This is known as yosei shoreikin ('encouragement money') and at the time of writing this was:

1. Yokozuna   ¥300,000
2. Ozeki   ¥200,000
3. Sekiwake   ¥100,000
4. Komusubi   ¥100,000
5. Makuuchi   ¥50,000
6. Juryo   ¥30,000

So, for example, if a heya has two makuuchi men, the master will receive ¥100,000 every basho.

14.30 Does the Kyokai provide assistance to the sekitori through the heya?

For each Tokyo basho a supplementary allowance of ¥25,000 is paid for each man of juryo level and above, officially to help with their clothing, hairdressing, and the like.

14.31 How and when did toshiyori originate?

Around the end of the 17th century, public performances were put on by a new class of former samurai. Often these were sumo ronin, that is, out-of-work retainers whose masters had lost their lands — and often their lives — in the civil wars. The more desperate became street-corner entertainers, putting on impromptu sumo displays; those seeking respectability and a more reliable source of income gathered together into informal business associations called kabu nakama and linked up with shrines and temples to put on kanjin-zumo, outdoor sumo tournaments designed to bring in money for the religious institution— with a cut for those who staged the event. By the middle of the 18th century the system had settled down into something like the sumo organization of today. The most famous of the retired men were the toshiyori, who acted not only as promoters and organizers but as judges.

14.32 When did sumo performances begin to receive official permission?

1684 is given as the first date. Public performances of sumo had been banned for the sake of maintaining public order, but a sumo ronin called Ikazuchi Gondayu obtained the permission of the Edo shrine magistrate to hold an 8-day kanjin-zumo tournament at the Fukagawa Hachiman Shrine in Fukagawa.

14.33 When did the sumo-beya system start?

It is partly a matter of definition. The rudiments of the modern system developed in the space of about 14 years from 1750. To organize public performances, retired rikishi and gyoji gathered together in a society called the Sumo Kaisho. Any house or building connected with the Kaisho came to be called a 'sumo room' — which is all that 'sumo-beya' means. But the sumo-beya as a place where rikishi lived and trained did not come into being until the latter half of the Meiji period, that is, about a hundred years ago. There was no direct development from the rikishi kept in the household of a great lord (daimyo) and those who pledged themselves to one toshiyori.

14.34 Have there always been 105 toshiyori myoseki?

By no means. This number dates only from the formation of today's (All-Japan) Sumo Kyokai in 1927, when the Tokyo and Osaka associations merged. It was a very unequal merger: to the 88 myoseki in the Tokyo Association, a mere 17 from Osaka were added. All the toshiyori names were originally the shikona of active rikishi; when they retired they simply kept their famous shikona; when the time came for them to designate a successor, the name, too, was passed on to him and thus became a myoseki.

Note: The number of myoseki has varied considerably. In the Horeki period (1751-64) there were 28; in the Tenmei period (1781-89), 39; this dropped to 32 in the Kansei period (1789-1801). In 1889 the Tokyo Association fixed the number at 88, to be joined in 1927 by the 17 from Osaka.

UNIT 15   DAILY LIFE

Section 1   SUMO-BEYA

15. 1 How many sumo-beya are there?

As of January 2003, there were 53, ranging from struggling little places in danger of winking out of existence because they had only one apprentice, to established heya with twenty-five or more.

15.2 Is there any rule about where they should be?

No, but it is not practicable for a heya to be too far from Ryogoku, or too isolated, ecause a long commute is not only tiring; it discourages rikishi from going out to train at other heya (de-geiko).

15.3 How are the living quarters divided up in a heya?

The lowest-ranking apprentices live together in a large tatami-matted room. They have mattresses (futon — still commonly used by ordinary Japanese), which they spread on the floor to sleep on at night and fold up and put away in large closets in the morning, leaving the floor clear. Each boy has his own box for his possessions, mainly changes of clothing. The rikishi of makushita level are usually allowed to use a smaller room, often the agari-zashiki, the raised seating area around the keikoba, for relaxation and sleeping. Only when a man is promoted to sekitori status is he entitled to a private room — one of the most prized rewards of success.

The master's family quarters are usually a suite of rooms in the same building.

If a rikishi marries, he is expected to move out and set up home with his new wife somewhere within easy commuting distance. He attends daily keiko and afterwards eats chanko lunch in the heya, but after that he goes home.

If the heya has unmarried gyoji or yobidashi, their accommodation depends on the size of the building; but ideally a young gyoji should be able to keep a little distance between himself and the rikishi of his own age, since he must exercise authority over them on the dohyo.

15.4 What is the timetable of a typical day in a heya?

1) Wake-up time
   Juniors   5:00—5:30
   Sekitori   7:00—7:30

2) Keiko time
   Juniors   6:00—9:30
   Sekitori   9:30—10:30

Note: These times are approximate, and sometimes the sekitori may join in with the juniors to give them extra training before moving on to sekitori-only bouts.

The youngest and lowliest of the apprentices get up first, remove the sacred symbols from the center of the training ring, sweep the sand over it, throw a little salt in, and start their own keiko. In a small heya, the master may supervise the entire training session, and may even put on his mawashi and take an active part; in a large heya he is likely to depute the training of the lower ranks to men in the sandanme and makushita divisions.

Before a man starts actual bouts, he must go through stretching and limbering exercises, and especially the two basic sumo exercises, teppo and shiko. All practical details of keiko will be dealt with in the next section.

3) Bath time and chanko time

Juniors	11:30—1:30
Sekitori	11:30—1:00

In principle, when the sekitori have finished keiko, they take a bath, attended by their tsukebito; have their hair dressed; and then sit down to chanko, still waited on by their attendants. The younger boys often have their hair dressed while their seniors' keiko is still going on, but they bathe and eat after the seniors have finished. The order is reversed, however, during hon-basho time, when the juniors who have bouts that day need to eat before the sekitori. Those whose bouts are at the very beginning of the day may fight on an empty stomach, and then return to the heya for chanko — or eat a packed lunch at the Kokugikan.

4) Afternoon nap

All rikishi sleep for at least half an hour, after the midday meal is cleaned up. Very few have any difficulty in dropping off instantly, for it has been a long morning and they have just had a heavy meal.

5) Free time

After the afternoon sleep, the juniors have to do chores - cleaning their own quarters, and in shifts cleaning the whole heya and doing the cooking; after their chores, they generally have the rest of the day free, unless they are needed as tsukebito.

6) Evening meal
Around 6:00 p.m.

This is not usually very exciting, and often the boys will treat themselves to a bowl of noodles later in the evening, when a vendor wheels his stall around to the heya.

7) Evening

Unless wanted for something, the rikishi are free. The sekitori may be invited out by sponsors, in which case they will take one or two tsukebito with them. Some stablemasters impose a curfew on the younger apprentices, but few would want to stay out late. They have to get up early again next morning!

15.5 Who does the cooking?

In a very small, new heya, it may be the master or his wife. In an established heya, the deshi at makushita level and below take turns. This duty is called chankoban. Those on duty have to do their own keiko first, and then they go to the kitchen to start preparing the noontime meal.

15.6 Are there no professional cooks in sumo?

If a man in the lower ranks has become a skilled cook, when it is time for him to quit the world of active sumo his master may keep him on as chief cook, chanko-cho. He then teaches and supervises the youngsters on chankoban.

15.7 Is training done at other times of day?

In principle, keiko is done only in the morning. Many rikishi do other forms of exercise on their own initiative, however: in gyms with up-to-date equipment, designed especially to make them stronger; or special exercises for suppleness.

15.8 Is there any difference in daily life during a basho?

They get up a little later, and generally do light keiko, just to warm up.

15.9 How far ahead of time do they arrive at the basho venue?

The sekitori in general arrive at least 30 minutes before the time of their dohyo-iri, and usually an hour earlier. The juniors who have only their bouts to think of must allow plenty of time in case of accidents or traffic delays, since if they fail to arrive in time for their bout, they forfeit the match. They commonly aim at arriving two hours before the estimated time of their bout. (If a junior rikishi is unavoidably delayed on the way and telephones the Kyokai office, he may have his bout postponed, but this cannot be done for a sekitori because of the tight schedule of the final bouts.)

15.10 After a bout, does a rikishi go straight back to his heya?

A sekitori has more freedom. He takes a bath at the Kokugikan and may either return directly to the heya or go out for a drink or two with his supporters first. The lower-rankers go straight back, unless they are required as tsukebito. In that case, they may remain in the shitaku-beya ready to dress their senior, and will wait there or watch the sumo from an upstairs seat until they are needed again.

On the other hand, a boy with an early bout may have several hours to wait before he is needed, so he may return to the heya for a time, All the juniors still have their assigned duties in the heya, which needs cooks and cleaners even during hon-basho.

Section 2 KEIKO

15.11 How often do they train?

Basically, there is a training session (keiko) every morning, with an occasional day off for the whole heya; and after a tournament ends, there is a week's holiday.

15.12 How long does a keiko session last?

It varies according to the custom of the heya, the number of rikishi it has, and also the time of year; but in general keiko will begin at about 6:00 a.m. and go on to 10:30 or even 11:00 a.m. But this does not represent the length of time that each man is training. The most junior apprentices get up first, sweep the ring and begin their own keiko under the supervision of men one or two divisions higher. When their turn is over, after about an hour, the next division higher begin their training. Those who have finished leave the keikoba to do their chores, cleaning or cooking; after which they return to watch the more advanced techniques of the seniors.

But considerable variation is possible on this basic pattern; in summer, for instance, enthusiastic youngsters may wake at five or even earlier and go down to the keikoba, in order to get more opportunities for keiko. When there are many apprentices, two divisions at a time may train together; and if the sekitori of another heya come around for joint training, the makushita rank may go to the other heya so that they may have more time for training at their level.

15.13 Do they have any warming-up exercises?

Yes; these are most important. There are two basic exercises: teppo, slapping the hands alternately into a polished tree trunk set upright in the ground while swinging the leg on the same side across to the other side (this encourages coordination and most importantly develops a powerful thrust); and shiko, raising the legs to the side alternately and bringing the feet down hard on the ground. This strengthens the thighs and legs and helps lower the center of gravity. These two exercises are supposed to be done 100 times minimum every morning.

15.14 What form does the actually training take?

There are several kinds of keiko:

1) moshiai-geiko: a group of equals trains together; after a bout they all rush forward shouting 'watashi! watashi!' (Me! me!) and the winner nominates his next opponent. This means that a man who keeps on winning remains in the ring and gets more practice. It also means that a man who does not want to train can rush forward, but not fast enough to be selected!

2) sanban-geiko: two men of roughly equal skill have a series of bouts together, maybe working on one particular point. This is indepth training done when there are not too many men training at once.

3) butsukari-geiko (bumping training) : when the time is up for the training of one division, this signals the finish. Senior men get into the ring one by one and each takes on a youth who has just finished keiko. The senior offers his chest and braces himself; the exhausted junior slaps his belt and rushes into him, trying to push him right across the ring and out the other side. After two or three tries, the senior rolls the junior over. Sometimes the junior will be forced to do this till he is well past the point of exhaustion; this is in fact 'favourable' treatment because they are showing him how to find his reserves of strength. Visitors may be very shocked to see this happening; but a man apparently being bullied in this way will often

achieve promotion in the very next basho.

4) monde morau (getting a massage): a highly skilled man, often a visiting ozeki or yokozuna, will take on a long series of less skilled men. He gets, in theory, a nice warm-up as well as a close look at any rising talent. It is customary for such a man to handicap himself by not rising to the tachi-ai, but to passively accept the other man's charge. Otherwise, the basis of all training is to practise with one's equals.

15.15 Why do some rikishi visit other heya for keiko?

To expand their experience, in principle. Especially, a promising young man in a small heya must go out to train with suitable partners. In the case of a very senior man such as a yokozuna, he is doing another heya a favor by turning up to give its sekitori a chance to train with him. In some ichimon ('family' group of sumo-beya) there is a strong tradition of training together. During jungyo time, when the sekitori and many of the oyakata are away on a provincial tour, it is also common for two or more heya in the same ichimon to combine their remaining deshi and have only one of the remaining oyakata to supervise.

15.16 What happens after a keiko session?

There are unwinding exercises to be done. More shiko (5.3) and, for the juniors, a set of simple exercises reminiscent of what they learned in the training school (1.21). Finally they all squat, close their eyes, and in a meditative way, they try to focus all that they have done that morning. After that, off they go to the bath and, eventually their first meal of the day — after they have first served their seniors in descending order!

UNIT 16   MONEY MATTERS

16.1 Do rikishi make a lot of money?

Compared with other sports such as baseball, the rewards of sumo are not particularly high. The reason lies in the fact that successful sekitori cannot transfer to a different heya in the way that baseball players or footballers can move to a different team. This means that there is no competition to drive up the price. All rewards in sumo are decided by the monolithic Nihon Sumo Kyokai, which can even debar all its members from taking some lucrative advertising jobs, and takes a percentage of such earnings in cases it has approved.

> Note: This chapter describes the 'money matters' from around 2001. Things have changed somewhat since then, but remain basically the same. The income of individual rikishi is not made public for reasons of privacy.

16.2 Can we find out how much a rikishi earns?

Some people might think that a man's income is a private matter; but the income of sumo wrestlers is laid down by the Kyokai and published in the press. But there are so many variables that it is extremely difficult to generalize about sumo incomes. Although the basic income is the same for everybody at the same rank, every man in the two sekitori divisions, for instance, receives a different amount of additional allowances.

16.3 Do all rikishi receive a monthly salary?

No; only the sekitori, that is, juryo and above. The heya system enables the

Kyokai to avoid paying regular salaries to the hundreds of rikishi in the four lower divisions. These get only a meager allowance every other month; but the stablemaster provides them with basic food, clothing and shelter, and seniors and admirers are expected to offer extras in the way of entertainment and gifts from time to time. But the whole sumo ethos is based on encouraging young men to strive constantly for promotion, and the sumo way of doing this is by making life hard at the bottom, and giving ever greater rewards to the man who rises through the ranks.

16.4 What was the origin of the salary system?

A modern salary system was introduced in May 1957, not only for rikishi and oyakata but for gyoji, yobidashi and other Kyokai employees. Up to then, there was a system called bukata-kin, in which the takings for each basho were divided out. The uncertainty of one's income made life difficult, so by general request the modern system was set up. Even earlier, in the Edo period, there was a primitive system called okanjo 大勘定 — the Great Reckoning. Twice a year all the sekitori and the oyakata would go to the office of the Sumo Kaisho (the predecessor of the Sumo Kyokai). All the profits for six months were piled in a heap and measured out, gold and silver coins together, in wooden measuring boxes called masu. Each man received one or more masu filled with coins, according to his status.

16. 5 What is the salary scale?

These are the figures as of January 2001, when there was a 3% increase for sekitori and oyakata. Declining ticket sales put the normally annual increase on hold in 2000 and again in 2002. The figures on the left are those for 1998.

o Sekitori

Rank	Basic salary	Allowance	Total 1998	Increase	New 2001
yokozuna	¥1,730,000	¥1,007,000	¥2,737,000	¥83,000	¥2,820,000
ozeki	¥1,440,000	¥838,000	¥2,278,000	¥69,000	¥2,347,000
sanyaku	¥1,080,000	¥563,000	¥1,643,000	¥50,000	¥1,693,000
maegashira	¥870,000	¥400,000	¥1,270,000	¥39,000	¥1,309,000
juryo	¥720,000	¥285,000	¥1,005,000	¥31,000	¥1,036,000

o Toshiyori

riji	¥1,120,000	¥285,000	¥1,405,000	¥43,000	¥1,448,000
kanji	¥990,000	¥242,000	¥1,232,000	¥37,000	¥1,269,000
iin	¥800,000	¥201,000	¥1,001,000	¥31,000	¥1,032,000
shunin	¥680,000	¥169,000	¥849,000	¥26,000	¥875,000
toshiyori	¥630,000	¥154,000	¥784,000	¥24,000	¥808,000
jun-toshiyori	¥630,000	¥154,000	¥784,000	¥24,000	¥808,000

o Director (riji)

Executive director (kanji)

Executive (yakuin taigu)

Committee member (iin)

Counselor (sanyo)

Manager (shunin)

Elder(toshiyori)

Jun-toshiyori (temporary toshiyori)

16.6 How much do the lower ranks earn?

They get basho-teate, an allowance paid each basho. The amount rises with the rank.

Makushita	¥120,000
Sandanme	¥85,000
Jonidan	¥75,000
Jonokuchi	¥70,000

They also get bonuses (shoreikin, incentive pay) depending on their showing in the last basho. It is calculated, like just about everything else in sumo compensation, in a unique and complicated way:

	makushita	sandanme	jonidan and below
kachiboshi	¥2,500	¥2,000	¥1,500
kachikoshiboshi	¥6,000	¥4,500	¥3,500

A kachi-boshi (hoshi - a white star) is a win; a kachikoshi-boshi is a win in a kachi-koshi score, that is, one with more wins than losses. Since rikishi in makushita and below have only seven bouts in 15 days, kachi-koshi is a score of four or better. So the calculation is done like this:

If a makushita rikishi has a score of 5-2, he gets 5 x ¥2,500 = ¥12,500; he also has two kachi-boshi, his fourth and fifth win, which bring him 2 x ¥6,000 = ¥12,000. Add the two together and his incentive pay comes to ¥24,500.

16.7 If a man is demoted, does his salary go down?

Yes; if a man goes down from makuuchi to juryo, he receives the juryo rate, although the amount of his hoshokin allowance (see 16.18 below) does not change. If he drops out of juryo into makushita, he loses his salary altogether, and no longer draws hoshokin money.

16.8 Do sumo people get regular raises?

The Directors of the Kyokai usually announce a 6% increase in salaries at the start of each year. This is in line with the expected increase of any other salaried workers. In 1992, however, they announced an increase of 56% in salaries for themselves and the sekitori. Although this was at a time when the Hanada brothers were rising stars and drawing a lot of publicity, the effect on the paying public cannot have been good, and already the cheaper seats were becoming easier to obtain except for the weekends. For 1998, they gave a raise of 10%, but returned to 6% for 1999. Declining popularity, combined with a business recession affecting sponsorship, led to a suspension of the expected increase both in 2000 and 2002.

16.9 Are there any extra allowances for the top men?

Yes, quite a number, depending on rank. Each basho, for instance, the title-holders receive a tokubetsu basho teate (special basho allowance):

yokozuna	¥200,000
ozeki	¥150,000
sekiwake	¥50,000
komusubi	¥50,000

Unlike the salary, this allowance is based on appearances, so it is cut if the man is absent from the basho. He gets the whole sum if he appears on 11 days or more; two-thirds if he appears from six to ten days; and one-third for up to five days. If the man does not appear at all he receives no tokubetsu basho teate.

16.10 What is hoshokin?

It is 'encouragement money,' a bimonthly allowance paid at hon-basho time to each sekitori which is based on his win/loss record going right back to his entry into sumo. He starts off with a basic entry of ¥3. A clerk in the Kyokai office updates the record on his page in a big file (and now, on a computer too, one assumes), entering his kachikoshi-boshi, the number of wins after kachi-koshi. Since the bottom four divisions have only seven bouts in a 15-day basho, kachi-koshi, or more wins than losses, is 4-3. For every win above 50% (three and a half!), he is credited with half a yen. So a 4-3 score gives him half a yen, 5-2 one yen, and a 7-0 record, two yen. If he has more losses than wins, nothing is deducted, but the total does not rise either. The total is called mochi-kyukin. But as yet he receives nothing; it is a figure on his record page. Throughout his career in the lower ranks the total will increase, but it will mean nothing unless and until he is promoted to sekitori rank.

Once he is a sekitori, the total of his mochi-kyukin means something, for it will be multiplied by 4,000 every basho and paid to him as an allowance. In any case, promotion to juryo means a minimum mochi-kyukin of ¥40. If his total has not reached that sum, he is credited with it anyway; if he has been a long time in the lower ranks and has more than ¥40 in his mochi-kyukin record, that is what he gets. So a new juryo gets a hoshokin allowance of ¥40 x 4,000 = ¥160,000. Similarly, on going up into makuuchi, a man's minimum mochi-kyukin is regarded as ¥60, so his hoshokin will be ¥240,000.

16.11 What else increases the mochi-kyukin?

Winning the yusho of one's division; and in makuuchi, winning the yusho adds ¥30, and a 15-0 zensho yusho adds ¥50, while a kinboshi for a rank-and-file man who defeats a yokozuna rates ¥10. All these small sums, remember, are multiplied by 4,000 when the allowance is paid.

16.12 Are there any other allowances?

There are out-of-Tokyo travel allowances, ryohi. which cover lodging and a per diem for expenses.

rank	lodging	per diem
yokozuna	¥8,000	¥3,000
ozeki	¥7,500	¥2,000
sanyaku	¥6,500	¥1,600
maegashira	¥5,700	¥1,400
juryo	¥5,000	¥1,200

Junior ranks, of course, have board and lodging provided in the heya's temporary camp.

16. 13 What are the one-off rewards?

1) The Kyokai gives a money prize to the champion of each division.

makuuchi yusho	¥10,000,000
juryo yusho	¥2,000,000
makushita yusho	¥500,000
sandanme yusho	¥300,000
jonidan yusho	¥200,000
jonokuchi yusho	¥100,000

2) The three special prizes, (sansho) each carry a money reward:

shukunsho,k kantosho, ginosho: ¥ 2,000,000 each.

If a special prize is awarded to two men, both get the full two million yen.

3) The Kyokai also pays meiyosho? meiyokin? for promotion to the top two ranks:

¥1,000,000 for promotion to yokozuna
¥500,000 for promotion to ozeki

Note: If an ozeki is demoted and later gets back to the same rank, he does not receive this allowance again.

16.14 Do the rikishi get a retirement allowance?

The sekitori receive a lump sum payment called yorokin, which is calculated according to rank and length of service.

There is also tokubetsu korokin, a payment in recognition of outstanding service to sumo. Some examples of this are:

Akebono	¥100,000,000	(1/2001)
Wakanohana III	¥70,000,000	(3/2000)
Asahifuji	¥20,000,000	(1992)
Hokutoumi	¥35,000,000	(3/1992)
Onokuni	¥25,000,000	(7/1991)
Chiyonofuji	¥100,000,000	(5/1991)
Takanosato	¥22,000,000	(1/1986)
Kitanoumi	¥50,000,000	(1/1985)
Wakanohana II	¥25,000,000	(1/1983)
Wajima	¥35,000,000	(3/1981)

| Taiho | ¥25,000,000 | (5/1971) |
| Tochinishiki | ¥2,000,000 | (1960) |

16.15 What are the envelopes a winner receives after a bout?

This is kenshokin, prize money that rides on the makuuchi bouts. Each envelope contains ¥60,000 (since May 1991), of which ¥30,000 is handed over in cash, ¥25,000 kept by the Kyokai to pay the rikishi's tax, and ¥5,000 taken by Kyokai for expenses.

16.16 Can anyone put up a kensho prize?

No, only an institution or a business.

16.17 What other income does a successful man have?

A yokozuna dohyo-iri is needed when a new sumo-beya is opened, and the fee for this is a million and a half to two million yen. Public appearances, for example, at autograph-signing sessions, has gone up in the last ten years or so from ¥300,000 to ¥1,000,000. A popular sekitori can spend every evening being wined and dined, and expects to receive at least ¥120,000, in new notes in a small envelope, tucked into the bosom of his silk kimono. (For this he is expected to talk pleasantly with the guests, pose for endless photographs, sign square cards, and, if sufficiently talented (or even when not), sing for his supper. Not for nothing are sumo men called 'male geisha,' a name that they hate. Shrines and temples also like to invite sumo celebrities as attractions for their festivals.

16.18 What kind of expenses does a sekitori have?

His day-to-day expenses may be high because he normally travels by taxi; he has also to wear silk kimono to parties and when going to or from the basho. His training mawashi, though cotton, is still expensive; and although his kesho-mawashi are gifts, his silk shimekomi (belt for tournaments) may not be — but he must still have one. He is also expected to tip such people as the tokoyama, hairdresser, from time to time, and to treat his tsukebito to food and drink (and sometimes female company). In other words, he is expected to share his winnings.

But if he wishes to stay in the sumo world after retiring from active competition, he must face the major task of raising the money to buy a myoseki, the stock that carries an elder's name and guarantees him a stake in the Sumo Kyokai until he retires at the age of 65. The sumo world has always been very secretive about the money that changed hands, but the current cost of buying a myoseki was defined by a lawsuit in 2003 as ¥175,000,000; previously the nearest guess had been ¥300,000,000!

If a retired man wishes to go independent and found his own heya, he must also find the money to buy a plot of land and to pay for the building itself.

UNIT 17 GETTING TICKETS

Section 1 SUMO-JAYA

17.1 What are the sumo-jaya?

They are the so-called tea-houses (chaya), some of which date from the early 19th century, that sell tickets for most of the ground floor sajiki (low, square enclosures with three, four, five or six cushions) and serve refreshments to their customers. Their official name is now the Kokugikan Service Company Ltd., and the twenty chaya in the Kokugikan have only numbers, not names; but old habits die hard, and in fact, their traditional names are still used by owners, employees, and sumo habitues. Some of the oldest trace their origins to the days when outdoor tournaments were held in the grounds of the Ekoin Temple in Ryogoku, close to where the first Kokugikan was built. The first chaya were simple booths made of reed mats hung from a wooden frame. Some were allowed inside the temple compound, while others were set up outside.

They were formerly independent, but when the first covered Kokugikan was opened in 1909 the Kyokai gathered the existing ones together in one place, just outside the building, and allowed another six to be added. Eventually they were all housed in one long building. In the Kuramae Kokugikan they were in small booths in one of the two entrances. Finally in 1957 the Kyokai and the chaya owners got together and set up a joint stock company, the Sumo Service Company. In a further change, the Kyokai turned the organization into the Kokugikan Service Company under its own aegis in January 1985, when the present Kokugikan opened. The chaya have an entrance all to themselves, to the left of the main entrance hall. The numbering starts with no. 1 on the right, and goes on in sequence down the right side, and back up the left; thus no. 20 faces no. 1.

Although the chaya may seem to be parasitic, since they control an overwhelmingly large number of the best seats, they serve the Kyokai as a buffer. When sumo is popular, there are many complaints against the chaya owners for their near-monopoly, which enables them to sell tickets at a small profit, along with refreshments and souvenirs that easily double the price of the seats. But sumo goes through hard times, too, and if the customers stay away, it is the chaya owners who are left with unsold seats and no customers wanting to buy refreshments and souvenirs. So the chaya take the loss and protect the Sumo Kyokai from financial disaster.

17.2 How many tickets do the chaya control?

About 70% of the downstairs seats '桝席.' Most of the balcony seats are on general sale, although the chaya have some of these too.

17.3 Do the chaya make a big profit from the tickets?

The Kyokai sells the tickets to the chaya at a 10% discount, so the profit is not large. The chaya make their profit from selling large bags of refreshments and sumo souvenirs (such as teapots, teacups, plates and bowls) to the customers.

17.4 Who are the people who work at the chaya?

Apart from the owners, who are mostly women, the most noticeable are the dekata, literally caterers. These are men who wear tattsuke-bakama cut-away pants just like those of a yobidashi. They guide customers to their seats, take their orders (the main package is already decided, but they can select what drinks they wish to have), bring the food and drink and clear up. The chaya also hire temporary workers, usually students, to help, and the lowly work of carrying heavy bags and clearing away empty bottles is usually left to them. It is the dekata, however, who expects a tip.

17.5 Can anyone become the owner of a sumo-jaya?

No; they are normally kept in the family, and in any case there is virtually always a sumo connection. Successful rikishi often marry the daughter of a chaya owner.

17.6 What are the names of the Tokyo chaya?

This is a list of the twenty chaya in Tokyo, giving the numbers by which they are officially known, the historic names that still cling to them, and a few points of interest.

1. Takasago-ya: dates from 1787, inside the Ekoin compound; started by a high-class woman married to a protege of the original Takasago.
2. Kinokuni-ya: originally outside the Ekoin compound; now run by widow of late Kagamiyama oyakata.
3. Yamato-ya: originally outside the Ekoin compound; Kasugano connection.
4. Yoshikawa: early 1900s; Izutsu connection; until her death the mother of the present Izutsu oyakata (Sakahoko) and Terao ran it with her mother.
5. Minokyu: started by a man who had worked for no. 14
6. Nakabashi-ya: Edo, inside Ekoin compound
7. Wakashima: established 1909
8. Joshu-ya: established 1909
9. Nishikawa-ya: about 1717 — one of the oldest; later, inside Ekoin ompound.
10. Mikawa-ya: established 1909

11. Josho: established 1909 by a dekata of no. 9

12. Yotsuman: Edo period; run by wife and mother-in-law of former Dewanoumi oyakata, Yokozuna Sadanoyama.

17. Musashi-ya: Edo period. Once patronized by a son and grandson of the 15th Tokugawa Shogun.

14. Shirato-ya: late Edo period

15. Hasegawa-ya: established 1909

16. Kawahei: Edo period

17. Fujishima-ya: early Meiji period

17. Isefuku: Edo period

19. Tatekawa: established 1909

20. Hayashi-ya: established 1909

17.7 Can anyone get tickets from a chaya?

Each chaya has its own regular customers. Especially for the front seats, which are mostly held by big companies, the connection may go back a very long way. But in the late 1990s as sumo declined in popularity to some extent, some of the chaya were indeed offering masu-seki for sale — though not at the front and not for weekends. In the 2000s they opened their own booking office to the left of the entrance (regular tickets are sold to the right), where their unsold tickets could be bought by the general public.

17.8 Are there chaya in Osaka, Nagoya and Fukuoka?

The system was discontinued in Fukuoka some years ago, but there are sixteen chaya in Osaka and seven in Nagoya. An eighth went out of business in Nagoya after 2001. They have local owners, and different names.

17.9 Is there any connection at all between the Tokyo and out-of-Tokyo chaya?

There is one connection: formerly about half the Tokyo dekata also went to work in Osaka and Nagoya. The other half were local people. In recent years, fewer men from Tokyo are going down and a greater number of local people are being employed. There is no one-to-one connection; the employees of one Tokyo chaya may go to several different chaya in Osaka and Nagoya.

Section 2 TICKETS

17.10 Without a connection to a chaya, how do I get tickets?

Through the ticket agencies: Playguide, JTB, Nihon Ryoko, Ticket Saison, Ticket Pia, the Kokugikan or the Gymnasium where an out-of-Tokyo basho is to be held, and, lately, through special machines in the 1,400 countrywide chain of Lawson convenience stores.

If you do not manage to get an advance sales ticket, it is possible to go along to the sumo stadium on the day you want to go, and buy a tojitsu-ken (same day ticket) for a moderate price. Normally 400-500 of these are on sale each day, from 9.00 a.m. If there are any advance sales tickets left for other days, these will also go on sale at the Kokugikan ticket window from 10.00 a.m.

17.11 What kinds of tickets are there?

They vary according to the type of seat and its position in the hall.

> Note: The details below refer only to the Kokugikan in Tokyo; elsewhere, the halls are made to resemble it as closely as possible but inevitably the details vary.

1) Tamari-seki (sunakaburi)

Don't even bother to ask; these six rows of single ringside cushions are very special, and only very special people have them. On television you will recognize the same people sitting in the same places, and this is because a seat in this area is 'owned' by one person. They are even passed down from father to son. Tamari seats are also sold for the whole basho, in booklets of fifteen.

2) Masu-seki (sajiki-seki) (A, B and C)

These are cushion (zabuton) seats in little 'boxes' separated from the rest by low steel railings. They most commonly seat four people, although there are ones on corners that hold fewer or more. Most of these seats are held by important supporters club members or big firms on an annual basis. The Sumo Kyokai sells 90% of them to the Sumo Service Company (sumo-jaya). The remaining 10% go on sale a certain number of weeks before each basho (the interval varies according to the venue).

3) Isu-seki (chairs), shitei (reserved) (A, B and C)

Upstairs in the balcony, the front six rows (A-seki) are comfortable red push seats with little tables on the arm-rests. Separated by a wide gangway, the next five rows (B-seki) are only slightly less plushy, but have no tables. Above them, and separated by another gangway, are three rows of C-seats. These are narrower and joined together; but they are still quite comfortable. Of these, the front two rows (rows 12 and 17) are reserved, and therefore available in advance sales.

4) Isu-seki (unreserved)

UNIT 17 GETTING TICKETS

Only the very last row is unreserved. These seats are available for those who buy tojitsu-ken, same-day tickets. (The unreserved seats are only those on the straight sides of the Kokugikan; the single row across each corner is, in, fact, row 12, and reserved.)

5) Places for wheelchairs

At the rear of each corner downstairs, there are two wide spaces which can accommodate wheelchairs or other special equipment. When not in use for the handicapped, a seating platform is wheeled into place and they are used as C masu-seki.

6) Box-seki

In the present Kokugikan, the very back row downstairs is something new: so-called box-seki (the English word 'box' is used) are walled enclosures containing a round table and five western-style swivel chairs. Although they are the furthest from the dohyo, they are popular because they are roomy and comfortable.

17.12 When does advance booking (maeuri) start?

It varies very much according to the place. They count back from the opening day of the basho.

Tokyo:	3-4 weeks before
Osaka:	4 weeks before
Nagoya:	4 months before!
Fukuoka:	5 weeks before

The Kyokai announces the dates for each year. and prints them all on the one-page calendar (given away free at the January basho) and in the Sumo Diary, on sale in the Kokugikan.

17.13 Can tickets be bought on the day?

Yes, 400-500 unreserved tickets are kept for sale on the day. The ticket office at the Kokugikan opens at 8.00 a.m. (but in other venues it is often 9.00) and same-day tickets (tojitsu-ken) are sold on a first-come, first-served basis, one only per person. For the middle Sunday and the final two days it is a good idea to arrive early, but spending the night on the street outside has never been really necessary. In times of high popularity these tojitsu-ken go very quickly and it is necessary to arrive at 6.00 a.m. or even earlier; but as of 1999, some have remained unsold even in mid-afternoon on weekdays.

17.14 How do we know when ticket sales will begin?

The Kyokai announces it on its own web site: <http://www.sumo.or.jp> in both Japanese and English. A week before advance booking starts, the Kyokai puts out posters, featuring either a woodblock print of a famous bout of the past, or a recent photo of rikishi in the news. There are usually announcements in the newspapers too, and certainly announcements in the sumo magazines. But if you look at the chart in 17.15, you can work it out for yourself.

UNIT 18   FOREIGNERS IN SUMO

18.1. How many non-Japanese have been rikishi?

It's a little hard to classify. For instance, Japan once annexed Korea, so technically Koreans counted as Japanese at that time. One of the most famous and successful of these, Rikidozan, isn't on the official list for that reason (and also because they were very much second-class citizens so he was quietly adopted by a Japanese couple while his stablemaster lied in his teeth about the origins of his young star). There are others who were born to foreign residents, both Korean and Chinese, in Japan. And while North Americans have not particularly distinguished themselves, several of the men from the island countries of the Pacific have had outstanding success; they are counted as 'Americans' but to classify them only by nationality would be misleading. Most of the Brazilians, some of whom have done quite well, are of Japanese ancestry and are easy to overlook, with their Japanese names and faces — though there was one with an Italian name (Pasquale Boschi) who stuck it out for a long time and got close to juryo. And how about Chinese? There have been Chinese rikishi from mainland China and Taiwan, as well as one from Hong Kong (who counted as a UK citizen at the time), as well as a man born in Osaka of Chinese parents. In the opposite direction, there's one Osaka man that everybody assumes is a foreigner, judging by his looks, but he is in fact a Japanese of mixed race who simply takes after his Indian grandmother. So making lists is a rather risky business, as the same man may appear on more than one list or someone else doesn't appear at all! Here, however, we will stick to the official record kept by the Sumo Kyokai.

18.2. When did the first foreigner enter sumo?

In 1934 an American of Japanese ancestry called Shoji Hiraga joined Kasugano-beya but did not get far despite trying for three years. After him, six other Japanese-Americans tried their luck before World War II, but only one was successful. Nobody else got higher than sandanme 22.

18.3 Who was the first successful American rikishi?

Harley Ozaki. A nisei (second-generation Japanese American) born on February 3, 1918 in Colorado, USA, he joined Dewanoumi-beya in January 1938 and fought under the name of Toyonishiki. He went right up to the top division, as far as maegashira 18. His career, though interrupted and badly affected by World War II, lasted from January 1938 to May 1944. After his retirement he remained a respected figure on the Tokyo scene and lived out most of his long life not far south of Ryogoku where for decades he kept a Japanese-style inn; he finally died in Kyushu on September 18, 1998, aged 78.

18.4 Who was the first successful non-Asian rikishi?

Without doubt, Jesse Kuhaulua, better known by his ring name Takamiyama, and more recently as Azumazeki oyakata. He arrived at Takasago-beya in March 1964, shivering in the first snow he had ever seen. He developed a simple method to succeed: exercise two or three times as much as the others. The highlight of his career came in 1972, when he took the championship at the Nagoya basho, the first foreigner ever to win a yusho. His highest rank was sekiwake, and he had an unusually long career, finally announcing his retirement in May 1984, just short of his 40th birthday. He had already become a Japanese citizen (since the Kyokai had made it a rule that only Japanese could hold myoseki and become oyakata), and in April 1986 he opened his own Azumazeki-beya. Although he was careful to recruit mainly Japanese (and seek his main support from Japanese sponsors), he continued his trail-blazing when his star recruit, a fellow-Hawaiian with the shikona Akebono, became the second foreign ozeki and, eventually, the first foreign yokozuna.

18.5 What area has produced the most foreign rikishi?

Until the late 1990s, the answer would undoubtedly have been the Pacific island countries, especially Hawaii, to which we should add Samoa, because some of the best, including the ozeki Konishiki and the yokozuna Musashimaru, were Samoan immigrants. Remember, too, that the population of these islands is ethnically very mixed. Akebono (Chadwick George Haheo Rowan) is a good example: his father Randy was Irish, Portuguese, Hawaiian, and Chinese, while his mother Janis was Hawaiian and Cuban. Musashimaru has some German in his ancestry. We may be forgiven for slipping into this list another American, Sentoryû (Henry Armstrong Miller), even though he was born in Japan and grew up in Saint Louis, Missouri. Otherwise he is on a list of one, being the only example of the racial mix of African-American father and Japanese mother.

At the turn of the millennium, however, the Americans were being rapidly overtaken by the Mongolians, and as of January 2003, a total of 36 Mongolians had come to Japan. This is exactly equal to all the Americans, if you lump mainland, Hawaii and Samoa together. Three of the original six Mongolians who came in 1992 quit almost immediately; but spurred on by the success of Kyokushûzan and Kyokutenho, they began to arrive in increasing numbers. Alarmed at this invasion of their ancient sport, the Sumo Association started talking about a ceiling of 18 men at any one time from each foreign country; but before a firm decision was made, the Mongolians had exceeded the number. So they tried a different tack: a limit of two foreigners in each stable, except for Oshima-beya which already had three Mongolians. (The point here is that you can't switch stables; a man can leave his stable only if he leaves sumo.) Since then the minimum has been lowered to one per stable — except, of course, in the case of those stables that already had three or two.

The influx of Mongolians has made the third group pale into insignificance. These are the Brazilians, who have numbered 13; the retirement of the one-basho juryo Wakaazuma in April 1803 leaves only two still active, of whom one is the veteran Kuniazuma. Since many of these Brazilians were of Japanese descent, neither their names nor their appearance are noticeably foreign. The most successful was Luis Go Ikemori, a 3rd-generation Japanese Brazilian in Tamanoi-beya who rose to juryo under the shikona Ryudo. He arrived in Japan in 1989 and entered Takushoku University, where he studied the Japanese language and then Business Management; as a freshman in November 1990 he became the 63rd college yokozuna, and the first foreigner to gain this honor. In 1996 he acquired Japanese nationality (coincidentally at the same time as Akebono).

18.6 What is the league table of all foreign rikishi?

As of 3/2003, it was:

US	36 (of whom 26 were Hawaiian) (2 active, of whom 1 naturalized — Musashimaru, Sentoryû)
Mongolia	36 including 1 waiting to enter (of whom only 4 have quit)
Brazil	13 (2 active — Kuniazuma, Azumao)
Taiwan	12
Korea	10 (2 active; but many more in the past were 'hidden' Koreans)
Tonga	6 + 2 = 8
China	6
Philippines	4 (but none of them lasted longer than a few weeks)
Russia	4 (of whom 1 is from Asian Russia)

Argentina	2 (1 active)
Samoa	2
UK	2 (including 1 Hong Kong Chinese)
Canada	1
Paraguay	1 (short time)
Sri Lanka	1 (left almost immediately)
Czech	1
Georgia	1 (promoted to juryo 5/03)
Bulgaria	1

So the total is 141 (and counting!), of whom 48 are still active. Those from the Philippines, UK, Paraguay and Sri Lanka weren't in long enough to be significant.

To put the 'active' numbers above in proportion, the total enrollment in professional sumo in January 2003 was 674. Thus the foreign-born contingent was fractionally over 14%. When you consider that in January 2001, exactly 2 years earlier, the figures were 716 and foreigners 28, and the proportion was just under 4%, this is a little worrying.

18.7 What happened to the six Tongan rikishi?

It is an unfortunate story. In 1974-5 a total of six young men joined Asahiyama-beya and made good progress.

When one of them, Tomonoshima, fought with Seattle sansei Bobby Suetsugu in Aki 1975 it was the first-ever bout between two foreign rikishi.

The stablemaster who recruited them died and there was a problem of who would take over. The widow wanted the heya to go to one oyakata, Ryuo, but the Kyokai approved another, Wakafutase. The Tongans' loyalty was with their master's widow and the new master one-sidedly 'resigned' them; the Tongans were forced to quit sumo. One of the six is now a pro-wrestler under the name Prince Tonga (Tonga is his real name), while another, Minaminoshima, regularly coaches an island amateur team which he takes to international meets. In March 2001, his son, also using the shikona Minaminoshima (his baptismal name, incidentally), passed maezumo in March 2001, along with another Tongan, Tevita Latu Laufa. Frankly they are not doing too well so far.

18.8 How many of the American/Pacific group have become sekitori?

So far, ten, mostly Hawaiian but including men of West Samoan birth or ancestry:

Yokozuna, two:
> Akebono (Chadwick George Haheo Rowan); father Randy was Irish, Hawaiian, Chinese; mother Janis was Hawaiian & Cuban.
> Musashimaru (Fiamalu Penitani) born W. Samoa, emigrated to Hawaii with family as ten-year-old

Ozeki, one:
> Konishiki (Salevaa Atisanoe) born in Hawaii of W. Samoan parents

Sekiwake, one:
> Takamiyama (Jesse Kuhaulua) Maui, Hawaii

Makuuchi, four (in order of highest rank attained):
> MW2   Nankairyu (Kiriful Saba), W. Samoa
> ME12   Yamato (Geo.Heywood Kalima), Hawaii
> MW12 (still active) Sentoryu, African-American/Japanese

Juryo, two:

JE5   Sunahama (Wm.Tyler Hopkins), Hawaii

W10   Daiki (Percy Pomaikai Kipapa), Hawaii

18.9 How many Caucasians have there been in sumo?

- Counting back from March 2003:
- Kagamifuji (Jason Walker, Texas 09/02-3/03), Kagamiyama
- Amuru   (Nicholai Ivanov, Russia, 05/02-), Onomatsu
- Hakurozan (Batraz Borazov, Russia, 05/02-), Hatachiyama
- Roho   (Soslan Borazov, Russia, 05/02-),Taiho
- Takanoyama (Pavel Bojar, Czech, 11/01-), Naruto
- Kokkai   (Tsaguria Merab Levan, Georgia,05/01-), Oitekaze
- Kuniazuma (Vander Ramos, Brazil, 09/91-), Tamanoi
- Sunahama (William Tayler Hopkins, Hawaii, 9/90-3/97), Takasago
- Koryu   (Eric Cosier Gaspar, Hawaii, 9/90-1/97), Takasago
- Hidenokuni (Nathan Strange, UK 9/89-5/90), actually only lasted till January but Jesse left him on the banzuke (dokisei of Musashimaru), Azumazeki
- Takamikuni (Taylor Wiley, Hawaii 3/87-7/89), Azumazeki

                    (1st foreigner to win makushita yusho)

- Kototenzan (John Tenta, Canada 11/85-5/86), Sadogatake
- Takanoumi (Philip Smoake, Texas 5/81-9/81), Taiho
- Wakatakami (Bryan George, Hawaii 7/77-11/83), Takasago
- Hakuzan   (Pasquale Boschi, Brazilian of Italian descent 3/77-5/86), Izutsu
- Muryu   (John Collins, Hawaii, 7/76-7/81), Futagoyama
- Araiwa   (Carl Martin, California, USA 11/68-9/71), Hanakago

18.10 How many Latin American countries have provided rikishi, and how have they fared?

Argentina, Brazil, and Paraguay. Many of these are men of Japanese ancestry and Japanese names, so they are often difficult to distinguish. Between 9/91 and 5/92, Ikemori and four other Brazilian nisei entered Tamanoi-beya.

Two Argentines in Michinoku-beya reached juryo: Hoshitango (Marcelo Salomon Imach, of Spanish-Jewish ancestry) and Hoshiandesu (Jose Antonio Juarez). The most successful Brazilian was Ryudo (Luis Go Ikemori), a third generation Japanese. He arrived in Japan 4/89, studied the Japanese language for a year at Takushoku University, then Business Management in the Commerce Dept. As a freshman in November 1990 he became the 63rd student yokozuna, the first foreigner top achieve this. His application for Japanese nationality was approved 22.4.96 (at the same time as Akebono's). Other Brazilian sekitori were: Wakaazuma (Kuroda Yoshinobu, one basho only) and Kuniazuma (Vander Ramos), both of Tamanoi-beya.

18.11 Since the war, how many men have come from other countries of Asia?

Let us separate the Mongolians, who now form a large group on their own, from other countries. Four have come from China and twelve from Taiwan; there was also, for a very short time, a Sri Lankan, and, for an equally short time, a Chinese from Hong Kong, who is officially recorded as a British national. A further complication is that the first Chinese sekitori, Kiyonohana (Liu Chao-hue) of Hanakago-beya, although officially from Taiwan, was recruited at his family's Chinese restaurant in Osaka. Another Taiwanese juryo was Tochinohana (Kasugano).

18.12 As of May 2003, how many Mongolian rikishi have there been?

A total of 36, of whom only three have quit. Originally Oshima oyakata (former Ozeki Asahikuni) recruited six young men; after a few months they all took refuge in the Mongolian Embassy, asking to be sent home. Eventually three were persuaded to return, and are still active; two are in the top division while one is still knocking around in the limbo between makushita and the top of sandanme. But encouraged by the success of Kyokushuzan, others started coming in from 1999, and in January 1803 Asashoryu (Dolgorsuren Dagvadorj) became the first Mongolian yokozuna.

18.13 Why did recruitment of foreign rikishi suddenly stop in the 1990s?

In early 1995, Dewanoumi Rijicho (now Sakaigawa oyakata) publicly announced the policy of 'enryo' ('voluntary restraint' on recruiting foreigners; actually none had been recruited for about two years before that time.

18.14 Is there now any limit on recruiting foreigners?

Yes; in 1998 there were a few new rules: an entrant must be able to operate in Japanese, and also the number of foreign rikishi is restricted to two per heya. An exception was made for Oshima-beya, which already had three Mongolians. But when the younger brother of one of them wanted to enter sumo, he had to go to a different heya (Fudoyama, younger brother of Kyokutenho, entered Takashima-beya). As increasing numbers of eager young Mongolians arrived in the year 2000, a further unwritten 'rule' surfaced: a maximum of 18 from any one foreign country. The Kyokai was not quick enough to decide, however, and by March 2001, 26 arrived.

18.15. Is there any limit on the race, nationality, or religion?

None whatsoever. It is possible, however, for a promising applicant to be deterred by some aspect of the sumo life. For instance, the Argentine Hoshitango is Jewish, but it would be quite impossible for him to maintain the kosher diet in a sumo-beya.

18.16 When a foreign rikishi retires, can he become an oyakata?

Apart from having the title to one of the 105 myoseki, the foreign-born rikishi must have one other qualification: Japanese nationality. This rule was brought in back in the 1980s when, for the first time, two non-Japanese looked as if they would qualify: the Hawaiian Takamiyama and the Japan-born Korean Kaneshiro. Fortunately the rule to keep them out was hastily devised and made no mention of birthplace: only Japanese citizenship was needed. Takamiyama promptly applied for naturalization, got it, and on retirement became Azumazeki oyakata. His star pupil, Akebono, became the first foreign yokozuna. (The unfortunate Kaneshiro fell ill and faded out of the world of sumo, so the question of buying a myoseki did not arise.)

Konishiki went through a nerve-racking period toward the end of his career when his application for citizenship took nearly a year to be processed — not an uncommon time, but in his case he had several close brushes with demotion that would have forced his retirement. If he had not had the necessary citizenship at the moment of announcing his retirement, he would have been barred from making use of the Sanoyama myoseki that he had already bought.

Determined not to be caught out in the same way, Akebono and the lower-ranked Ryudo (Ikemori, a Brazilian) put in their applications long before they expected to retire. Both came through in unusually quick time; about three months, in fact, in April 1996.

18.17 The foreign media often repeat Konishiki's claim that racism had prevented him from being a yokozuna. Is this true?

At the time when Konishiki was in line for promotion to ozeki, it is possible to make a case for this. And if he had been promoted earlier to sumo's second highest rank, he would have had more chances to get to the very top. It is a fact, however, that when he actually was an ozeki he never had the required 'two consecutive yusho or equivalent.'

18.18 What are some major landmarks?

1) 1964   Takamiyama's debut; first foreigner to win yusho 7/1972; retired as Azumazeki oyakata 1984 and founded Azumazeki-beya; as an oyakata he also served as sumo judge. He was the first foreign-born man to do any of these things.
2) 1987   Konishiki became the first foreign ozeki
3) 1993   Akebono became the first foreign yokozuna

Note: The two Hawaiian yokozuna, Akebono (64th, 1993.1-2001.1) and Musashimaru (67th, 1999.5-2—2004.11), were followed by five Mongolian yokozuna:

1) Asashoryu (68th, 2003.1-2010.1)
2) Hakuho (69th, 2007.5-2021.9)
3) Harumafuji (70th, 2012.9-2017.11)
4) Kakuryu (71st, 2014.3-2021.3)
5) Terunofuji (73rd, 2021.9 ~)

BIBLIOGRAPHY

• English language

Adams, Andy & Newton, Clyde, Sumo, London: Hamlyn, 1989.

Bickford, Lawrence, Sumo and the Woodblock Print Master, Tokyo: Kodansha International, 1994.

Cuyler, Patricia, Sumo from Rite to Sport, Tokyo: Weatherhill, 1985.

Hall, Mina, The Big Book of Sumo, Berkeley, California: Stone Bridge Press, 1997.

Newton, Clyde, Dynamic Sumo, Tokyo: Kodansha International, 1994.

Patmore, Angela, Sumo, London: Queen Anne Press, 1990.

Schilling, Mark, Sumo: A Fan's Guide, Tokyo: The Japan Times, 1994.

Shapiro, David, Sumo: A Pocket Guide, Tokyo: Tuttle, 1995.

Sharnoff, Lora, Grand Sumo, Tokyo: Tanko-Weatherhill, 1989; updated paperback, 1993.

Watson, Lyall, The Channel Four Book of Sumo, Tokyo: London: Sidgwick & Jackson, 1988.

• Japanese language

Edozumo-nisikie, (VANVAN Sumokai, Shinshun-go), Baseball Magazine-sha, 1986.

Furukawa, Sanki, Edojidai-no-ozumo, Kokumin-tairyoku-taikai, 1942.

Hikoyama, Kozo, Sumodo-sokan, Nippon-tosho-senta, 1977.

Hitachiyama, Taniemon (ed.), Sumo-taikan, Hitachiyama-kai, 1914.

Ikeda, Masao et al (ed.), Shashin-zukai-sumo-hyakunen-no-rekishi, Kodansha, 1970.

Ikeda, Masao, Sumo-no-rekishi, Heibon-sha, 1977.

Ikeda, Masao, Ozumo-monosiri-cho, Baseball Magazine-sha, 1998.

Kitade, Seigoro, Ozumo-e-no-shoutai, Kosaido, 1977.

Kitade Seigoro (ed. supervision). Naruhodo-zumo! PHP Kenkyusho, 1993.

Kokugi-sumo-no-subete, Bessatsu sumo-shukigo. Baseball Magazine-sha, 1980.

Kubodera, Koichi. Nihon-sumo-taikan. Shinjinbutsu Orai Sha, 1992.

Nema, Hiromi, Ozumo-gyojino-sekai, Yoshikawa-kobun-kan, 2001.

Nema, Hiromi, Kuwashikunaru-ozumo, Senshu University Press, 2020.

Nema, Hiromi, Ozumogyojino-sho'oto-shihonbashirano-shishoku, Senshu University Press, 2021.

Nema, Hiromi, Ozumono-gyojito-kaikyu, Senshu University Press, 2022.

Nihon Sumo Kyokai (ed.), Sumo- daijiten, Gendaisho-kan, 2002.

Nitta, Ichiro, Sumo no Rekishi, Yamakawa-shuppan-sha, 1994.

Sakai, Tad amasa. Nihon-sumo-shi, Baseball Magazin-sha, 1956/1964.

Showa-no-ozumo-kanko-iinkai (ed.), Showa-no-ozumo, TBS Buritanika, 1990.

Sumo-henshubu (ed.), Ozumo—jinbutsu-daijiten, Baseball Magazine-sha, 2001.

Sumo-ukiyoe (Bessatsu-sumo-kakigo), Baseball Magazine-sha, 1981.

Totani Taichi (ed.), Ozumo. Gakushu kenkyusha, 1977.

Tsuchiya, Yoshitaka, Sumo, Hosei-daigaku Press, 2017.

Wakamori, Taro. Sumo-ima-mukashi, Kawaide-shobo-shinsha, 1963.

Yamada, Inosuke, Sumo-taizen, Hattori-shoten, 1901.

INDEX

Y

Z

Introduction of the two authors

Doreen Simmons

A native of Nottingham, England, city of Robin Hood. Resident in Tokyo since 1973, and in Ryogoku, the sumo heartland, since 1978; former Classics teacher, now works directly and indirectly for the Japanese government. To keep sane, devotes much (but not all) of her spare time to an intensive study of sumo. Has written a bimonthly sumo column for the Kobe-based magazine 'Kansai Time Out' since 1983, and has been appearing regularly as a color commentator on NHK's 2-hour live satellite telecasts since 1992, when the service started. Wrote regularly for 'Sumo World' magazine for about ten years; as a feature writer has been published in the Okura Lantern, Asian Art, etc. Has been interviewed for the BBC, National Public Radio and other radio and TV broadcasters.

Note: Ms. Simmons was awarded the Orders of the Rising Sun (Kyokujitsusho, 旭日章) by the Japanese government in 2017. She died in April 2018.

Hiromi Nema

Hiromi Nema was a professor of English at Senshu University, Tokyo, and retired in 2013. He received a Master of Arts degree in TESL from St. Michael's College, Vermont, in 1968, and an MA in Linguistics from the University of Hawaii in 1974. Mr. Nema specializes in English phonetics and phonology. He has authored and coauthored many books in these fields, and books about sumo (fourteen books). His publications about sumo include, for example, Kokomade Shitte Ozumo-tsu (Graph Co., 1998), Sumo: 258 Key Questions (Yohan publisher, 1998) and Kuwashiku-naru Ozumo (Senshu University Press, 2020).

Japanese Sumo: Q & A

2022 年 10 月 31 日　第 1 版第 1 刷

著　者　　Doreen Simmons & Hiromi Nema

発行者　　上原　伸二
発行所　　専修大学出版局
　　　　　〒 101-0051　東京都千代田区神田神保町 3-10-3
　　　　　株式会社専大センチュリー内　電話 03-3263-4230
印　刷　　モリモト印刷株式会社
製　本

ISBN978-4-88125-374-8

Books published by Senshu University Press

『大相撲行司の伝統と変化』、2010
(Ozumogyoji-no-dento-to-henka)

『大相撲行司の軍配房と土俵』、2012
(Ozumogyoji-no-gumbaifusa-to-dohyo)

『大相撲の歴史に見る秘話とその検証』、2013
(Ozumo-no-rekishi -ni-miru-hiwa-to-sonokensho)

『大相撲行司の房色と賞罰』、2016
(Ozumogyoji-no-fusairo-to-shobatsu)

『大相撲行司の軍配と空位』、2017
(Ozumogyoji-no-gumbai-to-ku'i)

『大相撲立行司の名跡と総紫房』、2018
(Ozumotategyoji-no-myoseki-to-soshibusa)

『詳しくなる大相撲』、2020
(Kuwashiku-naru-ozumo)

『大相撲行司の松翁と四本柱の四色』2020
(Ozumogyoji-no-sho'o-to-shihonbashira-no-shishoku)

『大相撲の神々と昭和前半の三役行司』、2021
(Ozumo-no-kamigami-to-showazenhan-no-sanyakugyoji)

『大相撲の行司と階級色』、2022
(Ozumo-no-gyoji-to-kaikyushoku)